Uncertain Destiny

Stories and Memories of One Family's Journey in South Texas

Randy Krinsky

With contributions by
Rosa Nava Krinsky

Fulton Books, Inc.
Meadville, PA

Published by Fulton Books 2020

ISBN 978-1-64654-543-8 (paperback)
ISBN 978-1-64654-544-5 (digital)

Printed in the United States of America

Contents

Acknowledgments

If you would've asked me ten years ago if I could ever see myself writing a book, I would have laughed. It's a daunting undertaking and yet one of the most fulfilling experiences you can ever have. Of course, none of this would have been possible had it not been for my mother, Rosa Nava Krinsky. It was her initial idea to expand a short essay I wrote for a scholarship into a book (I won the award, by the way). Without her help, input, guidance, and financing, I could never have written this.

To Courtney Stevens, my trusty intern, research assistant, good friend, and partner in all this. She was priceless in helping me locate and obtain the research I needed to finish this book. I never could've done it without her!

When writing this book, I remembered all the great experiences I had with my family in Rockport. Though they are no longer with us, I will be eternally grateful for the love and kindness of my uncle Hector Nava Sr. (he'd give you the shirt off his back if you needed it), my uncle Daniel Garcia (a great patriot, a great soldier, and a great man), and my uncle Felix "Lito" Garcia (a proud ship's captain and a proud family man).

To Stela Moreno and everyone at Subject Matter Expert Translation LLC. Their help in transcribing and translating two-hundred-year old documents was invaluable! Also, many thanks to Cristela Cantú and Robert Tarín for their translation help too!

Writing a book about your family's generational journey is a fun but challenging and costly task. I'm forever indebted to everyone who helped fund my research trips: Dr. Nancy Lopez, Dr. Aaron Gillette,

Jason Rivas, Itzayana Lopez, Christine Barr, Claudia Preston, Roger Pollard, and my dear aunt Norma Garza!

A second shout-out to Courtney Stevens and Jason Rivas for their editorial assistance and ongoing support in helping see this dream through to the end. A special thank you to my talented graphic designer, Elaine Anita de Melo Gomes Soares.

Thanks to everyone else whose encouragement and support have allowed me to leave this work as a testament to my family and our legacy. To my dear father, Charles Victor Krinsky, I love you and miss you every day.

I dedicate this book to my grandparents, Rudy and Clara Nava, a pair of hardworking young kids who raised an incredible and beautiful family. We love you always!

The Journey Begins

The journey of Salvador Rodriguez and his family, my family, to Texas began years earlier in 1689 when a Spanish expedition located the destroyed French colony of Fort Saint Louis near what is today Inez, Texas. Spain had long claimed ownership of that territory as part of the Viceroyalty of New Spain. However, the Spanish government had not tried in earnest to settle the area. That all changed after the discovery of Fort Saint Louis. Fearing encroachment by the French presence in neighboring Louisiana, Spain decided to colonize Texas and set up missions.

Due to resistance by the native tribes, Spain abandoned colonizing efforts for the better part of two decades, until 1716.[1] Understanding that the French still posed a threat to Spanish land claims, Spanish authorities intended to strengthen their claim to Texas by stepping up settlement efforts and establishing several more missions and a presidio. The Spanish viceroy, Don Fernando de Alencastre, first duke of Linares, directed Martín de Alarcón, then governor of Coahuila y Tejas, to ultimately establish a mission in what is today San Antonio.[2]

Alarcón set out on an expedition and ended up near the banks of the San Antonio River. He met with a Franciscan priest, Fray Antonio de Olivares, and with the help of local Payaya Indians, construction began on the Misión de San Antonio de Valero (the Alamo), so named after Saint Anthony of Padua and the new viceroy of New Spain, Don Baltasar de Zúñiga y Guzmán, marquess of Valero.[3,4] On May 1, 1718, Alarcón ceded ownership of the completed mission to Fray Antonio de Olivares. Four days later, Alarcón commissioned the building of the Presidio San Antonio de Béxar roughly three-quarters of a mile away on the west side of the San Antonio River. Work also began on the Acequia Madre de Valero, the irrigation canal that would divert and control the flow from the San Antonio River, vital for crops and as a water supply to the area.[5,6]

The new settlement soon became a target for raids by the Lipan Apache Indians. The missionaries attempted to convert the East Texas Native Hasinai tribe but failed; however, this did lead to friendly relations between the tribe and the Spanish. The Hasinai, or the Tejas, from the Caddo word for *friends*, as the settlers called them, were the enemy of the Lipan Apache, who now shifted their hostilities toward the Spanish.[7] Repeated raids by the Apache took its toll on the livestock, with approximately one hundred animals taken annually.[8] Spain reasoned that an increased settler population willing to defend their property would deter Apache raids and reduce the costs of sending additional soldiers to the presidio.[9]

On February 14, 1719, José de Azlor y Virto de Vera, the marquess of San Miguel de Aguayo, proposed a plan to Spain's King Felipe V. Four hundred families should be resettled in the New Spain province of Texas. The families should come from colonies such as the Canary Islands, Galicia, or Havana. The king agreed, and his plan was approved. A notice was sent asking for two hundred families to volunteer from the Canary Islands.[10]

Most of those that volunteered, forty-four to be exact, were from the island of Lanzarote. This was chiefly because Juan Leal Goráz was head of the *cabildo*[11] of Teguise, which was on Lanzarote. Goráz had been charged by the captain general of the Canary Islands with the daunting task of gathering potential emigrants to satisfy the king's plan. The remaining volunteers were assembled from the other islands of La Palma, Tenerife, Gran Canaria, and Fuerteventura.

Lanzarote, the easternmost of the Canary Islands, sits in the Atlantic Ocean approximately 78 miles (125 kilometers) off the coast of the African coast. Mother Nature was harsh toward Lanzarote. The island was birthed from volcanic upheavals, and the landscape was left rocky and rugged. Only the sturdiest of inhabitants could call it home. As nature would have it, the first islanders became known for being just as robust as their home. The first Spanish to visit the island referred to the islanders as *Guanches*. The *Guanches* were a light-skinned, light-haired people. The inhabitants of the other islands, some referred to as *Majoreros*, were dark-skinned with dark hair. The Spaniards conquered the Canary Islands in the fifteenth century, leading to an intermixing of Spanish and native islanders. Roman Catholicism spread over the islands, replacing the indigenous superstitious rites and beliefs of the *Majoreros* and *Guanches*.[12]

One of the Catholic elders, Father Diego, spoke to a group of islanders and expressed his hope that many would volunteer. Though the final destination of the first emigrants to New Spain was unknown, it was his desire that they would settle near one of the newly completed missions near the San Antonio River. He believed the location would be idyllic, and the land was reported to be rich and fertile. The water from the river was clean, and a nearby stream could also be used for irrigation. This water supply could furnish the missions and the settlers with all they would need for successful farming and the raising of livestock. If Father Diego's grand vision for the new settlement wasn't enough to convince the islanders, he would also attempt to appeal to their sense of pride:

> You ought to enlist as volunteer settlers in Texas if for no other reason than to uphold the tradition of these ancient islands, which have been the starting point of every important voyage of discovery or development in the western world up to this moment.[13]

He would go on to recount how Christopher Columbus had stopped at Grand Canary Island in 1492 on his way westward into the unknown. Hernán Cortés also made port in the Canaries in 1504 on his way to Hispaniola. Even the English continued to the west using the Canaries as a launching point, with Captain Christopher Newport carrying the settlers from the Virginia Company on their way to establish the settlement of Jamestown in 1607. He would continue that the journeys of Columbus and Cortes brought glory to the Spanish kingdom but that the English were there only to strip the lands of their riches and dishearten the unfortunate Indians.

> The Lord be praised that the country open to you in the province of Texas is far removed from that occupied by the English. The French country, however, borders New Spain on the east, and our great sovereign's main purpose in colonizing the new province of Texas is to check invasions of Frenchmen upon Spanish territory. The forces of the French in Louisiana are small, and you need have no fear that the Spaniards will again allow them to enter New Spain. I urge you to accept our great King's offer to colonize in Texas.[14]

The chosen destination for the intrepid new settlers would be a small villa on the banks of the San Antonio River. Approximately thirty-eight soldiers and their families called the villa home, along with a few hundred natives, mostly from the Coahuiltecan tribe who lived at the Mission San Antonio de Valero. The Franciscan monks at the mission, along with two other missions in the area, tended to the religious conversion of the natives. The area missions were also responsible for overseeing the tending of the cattle, a forerunner of the ranching industry that would boom in the area in the years to come. These new settlers from the Canary Islands would be undertaking a whole new way of life.

By late January 1730, twenty-five families, most of which were from the island of Lanzarote, had volunteered. They would set sail from Santa Cruz, on the island of Tenerife, on March 27. Don Bartolome attended a special mass and appealed to the volunteers to be bold and loyal in hopes of finding peace and prosperity in their new homes. After calling out the last names of each of the volunteers, Don Bartolome went ashore and watched as the ship, the *España*, moved from the port. Don Bartolome bowed his head and kneeled. He crossed himself as the ship drew into the distance.[15]

The journey was long and arduous, and by June 1730, the twenty-five families from the Canary Islands had reached Havana, Cuba. Ten families chose to remain in Havana, while the rest continued their journey. After a year over sea and land, the weary travelers finally landed in Veracruz on July 19, 1730.[16] They traveled to Mexico City and then northward to Cuautitlán, an ancient Aztec village. It was there that Don Francisco Domingo de Lana, chief *alcalde*, or mayor, welcomed the islanders and allowed for them to rest and resupply. Under authorization from Don Juan de Acuña, the marquess de Casa Fuerte, Viceroy of New Spain, himself under orders from the king of Spain, made ready provisions for the new settlers to aid them in completing their journey. An official letter, dated November 9, 1730, signed by Don Francisco and attested to by royal official Don Manuel Angel de Villegas Puente, indicated that on November 6, he oversaw the distribution of clothing, arms, and other supplies. As it pertains to the Rodriguez family, he lists the dispersal as the following:

Salvador Rodriguez received two shirts, two white trousers, two jackets, two cravats, a cape, a riding coat, two pairs of woolen socks, two pairs of shoes, and a hat. He was given two horses, a saddle with stirrups and saddlebags, a bridle with headstall and reins, a *jáquima*[17] with its halter, two sheepskins, and a pair of spurs with their straps. He was issued a pair of boots, a broad cavalry sword, a belt, a knife, a gun with its holster, a girdle with its powder flask and corresponding gunpowder, balls and flints, a mattress, two sheets, a pillow with pillowcase and covering, a quilt, a packsaddle, and a copper pot with a lid (which also served as a frying pan).

María Perez Cabrera received two shirts, two white petticoats, two jackets, two handkerchiefs, two pairs of silk stockings, two pairs of understockings, two pairs of shoes, a petticoat made of serge (durable twilled wool), a white cloak, a shawl, and an upper petticoat. Like Salvador, she also received two horses, a saddle with saddlebags, a bridle with reins and headstall, a *jáquima* with its halter, and two sheepskins.

Patricio Rodriguez received two shirts, two pairs of white trousers, two jackets, two cravats, a cape, a riding coat, two pairs of woolen socks, two pairs of shoes, a hat, and a blanket. He also was issued two horses, a saddle with stirrups and saddlebags, a bridle with reins and headstall, a *jáquima* with its halter, two sheepskins, a pair of spurs with their straps, a pair of boots, a broad cavalry sword, a belt, a knife, a gun with holster, a girdle with its powder flask, and corresponding gunpowder, balls, and flints.[18]

As a group, the islanders were issued, for use as seen fit by Juan Leal Goraz, two axes, two hoes, two *machetes*, two small crowbars, ten saws, ten adzes,[19] ten chisels, twenty plowshares, ten *comales*,[20] and ten field tents.[21]

On November 8, 1730, under the authority of the viceroy, Don Juan, marquess of Casa Fuerte, a representative undertook an official accounting of the islander families. At that time, they consisted of fifteen families and four single men who were grouped together officially as the sixteenth "family." The total persons listed numbered fifty-six.

The Rodriguez family was officially listed as the eighth family and consisted of Salvador and Maria Rodriguez, both aged forty-two, and their son, Patricio, aged fifteen. The others listed were the families of, in order, Juan Leal Goraz, Juan Curbelo, Juan Leal, el Mozo Antonio Santos, Joseph Padron, Manuel de Niz, Vicente Álvarez Travieso, Francisco de Arocha, Antonio Rodriguez, Joseph Leal, Juan Delgado, Joseph Cabrera, Maria Rodriguez-Provayna, and Mariana Meleano. The sixteenth family was made up of the four adult, unmarried men: Phelipe Perez, Joseph Antonio Perez, Martin Lorenzo de Armas, and Ignacio Lorenzo de Armas. Each of the fifty-six persons making up the sixteen families was paid eighteen pesos, equivalent to two months of advanced wages.[22]

The islanders remained in Quantitlan until November 15, when they continued on their challenging journey towards their new home on the San Antonio River. The Spanish government had mapped out their traveling route, leading them through San Luis Potosi to the villa of Santiago del Saltillo de la Nueva Vizcaya, where they arrived on January 28, 1731. Captain Don Mathias de Aguirre greeted them. Having found the group of weary settlers to be short of provisions, losing their horses to exhaustion, and loaned mules returned to their owners, he notified the group that he had been authorized by the viceroy to restock their supplies adequately. In total, eighty-six horses were given to the group, alongside seventy-seven mules, loaded with provisions to sustain them for the rest of their journey. Of those mules, twenty-seven were loaded down with meat, biscuits, and other foodstuffs; also, four mules were used to carry four *cargas de arganas*, or panniers.[23] Additionally, sixteen yokes of oxen were given, one for each family and one for the group of single men collectively referred to as the sixteenth family.[24]

They continued on their journey traveling north ever closer to their new home, stopping at the Presidio of San Juan Bautista on the Rio Grande where their exhausted horses were left behind. As they grew nearer their destination, the sound of bands of Indians could be heard yelling in the distance. One particular night, near the end of their journey, the islanders were awoken by the sound of frightened horses and restless oxen. Indians had entered the camp of the sleeping travelers and were making away with horses. This raid, believed to be perpetrated by Karankawa tribesmen, took its toll on the frightened islanders. The women and children were frantic, and the men alarmed. That same night, a request was made by messenger to Captain Juan Antonio Pérez de Almazán of the Presidio at San Antonio de Béxar, requesting he send soldiers with haste. Captain Almazán dispatched twenty cavalrymen to guard the new settlers and escort them the final night and day of their journey.

In the early morning hours of March 9, 1731, the islanders began to undertake the last few miles of their trek from the Canary Islands to San Antonio de Béxar. By approximately 11:00 a.m., the wide-eyed new settlers had finally crossed the San Pedro Creek and made their way through the stockade gate that surrounded the fort, today known as San Antonio's military plaza. It had been nearly a year since they left their homes in hopes of a new start in a new home.[25]

The new settlers, led by Juan Leal Goraz, presented themselves to Captain Almazán. They checked in the equipment they had been issued by Captain Aguirre previously in Saltillo. Captain Almazán received the supplies and stock goods from them as detailed in a letter received from Captain Aguirre. As a group, the settlers returned all the tools and implements, and Salvador Rodriguez, along with the heads of the other families, checked in all the equipment he and his family were issued, except for seven horses. Those horses were thoroughly worn out and had been left behind in various locations along the route.

Don Juan Antonio Bustillo y Ceballos, governor of the Spanish colony of Texas, ordered that the new settlers quarter in whatever housing may be available once they arrive at the presidio. He further ordered that current residents should assist in the caring for and tending to the islanders' horses, oxen, and other animals until such a time that the new settlers had been taught how to tend to their livestock on their own. Every effort was to be made to ensure that the new settlers and their stock enjoyed all bounty of their lands and received all the assistance they would need to make a successful transition. Each of the fifty-six settlers would also receive four *reales* per day, roughly fifty cents, for the period of one year to help cover the costs of food and supplies as needed. This was so decreed by the governor and put into writing in a letter dated November 28, 1730, addressed to Captain Almazán.[26]

This letter, sent by Bustillo to Almazán, also contained a decree by the marquess de Casa Fuerte, Viceroy of New Spain. This viceroyal decree, also dated November 28, 1730, as read by the captain, honored the settlers, proclaiming them and their descendants, from that point on, as *Hijos Dalgo*, landholding nobility commonly known as *hidalgos*, "with all the honors and prerogatives that all landed nobles and knights of these kingdoms of Castille should have and enjoy, according to the laws and privileges of Spain." This allowed for Salvador Rodriguez and his son to be known by the style Don Salvador and Don Patricio.[27]

The site of their new homes was found and planned on a low, flat hill not far from the presidio. The settlement would be named La Villa de San Fernando, in honor of Don Fernando, a Spanish prince, and the future King Ferdinand VI.[28]

On July 20, 1731, Juan Leal Goraz, as the eldest and most respected of the settlers, was appointed the first *regidor*, or councilman. Salvador Rodriguez was named the fourth *regidor* of a group of councilmen that totaled six. A system was devised to have an *alcalde* to administer justice and administrate the villa. Within two weeks, on August 1, an election was held, and Goraz was formally elected *alcalde*. This was historic as it was the first election in the first civil settlement in the Spanish province of Texas, creating the administration of the first municipality "legally and officially recognized by the highest authority in New Spain."[29]

With their newfound status as *hidalgos*, the other residents of the villa begrudged the islanders, or *Isleños*, their status and privileges.[30] The *Isleños*, accustomed to farming, were not very proficient with horses and knew nothing of ranching. Their reluctance to build fences was often the cause of many quarrels with their neighbors as their livestock would sometimes trample through their fields.[31] By the early 1740s, the divide between the original settlers and the new *Isleños* narrowed as intermarriage and the necessity for closer community economic bonds became apparent. Additionally, original settlers were soon allowed to serve in municipal roles and as *regidors*.[32]

By December 31, 1788, the first formal census was conducted and referred to the municipality as the Villa de San Fernando, with the villa, surrounding settlements, the mission (commonly referred to now as the Alamo), and the presidio collectively known as San Antonio de Bexar. In 1832, Spain was ousted from Mexico, and Texas was divided into five separate regions with San Antonio de Bexar as the capital of the entire Texas province. Soon after, in 1836, the Republic of Texas Constitution reorganized the old settlements into counties, with San Antonio de Bexar lending its name to the new Bexar County. The county seat was to be the villa, which had now grown. The area's name was simplified to San Antonio on June 5, 1837, and later, on December 14, 1837, became officially the city of San Antonio.[33]

In 1971, the Texas State Historical Survey Committee, later renamed the Texas Historical Commission, authorized a historical marker to be placed in the main plaza, between San Fernando Cathedral and the Bexar County Courthouse. It denoted the site where the *Isleños* completed their five-thousand-mile journey and made a new home.

The *Isleños*, including Don Salvador and his family, founded what would ultimately become the seventh largest city in the United States. Though the journey was arduous and the life they volunteered for was hard, they willingly chose to leave their island and start a new life in what would be a new world for them. Today, all *Isleños* are remembered for the sacrifice they made and the legacy they left.

Title of Nobility Granted to Male Canary Islanders of San Antonio, Texas, and their Descendants in Perpetuum

What follows is a translation of a portion of a certified copy of the instructions to Bustillo y Bustamante as given by the viceroy of Spain, Juan de Acuña, marquess de Casa Fuerte, dated November 28, 1730, concerning the arrival of the Canary islanders. This certified copy rests in the Bexar Archives of the Dolph Briscoe Center for American History, San Antonio, Texas.

Translation is as given.

In law 6, title 6, book IV, of the summary of the Laws of the Indies, His Majesty states the following:

> In order to honor any persons and their children, or legitimate descendants, who may undertake to found settlements, when they have concluded and established such settlements, we hereby make them land-holding nobles, (Hijos Dalgo de Solar Conocido), so that in that settlement and in any other part of the Indies they may be known as land-holding nobles (hijos dalgo) and persons of noble lineage and estate, (solar conocido); and, in order that they be known as such, we hereby grant them all the honors and prerogatives that all landed noblemen and knights of these king-

17

doms of Castile should have and enjoy, according to the laws and privileges of Spain.

Therefore, by virtue of this law, His Majesty shall declare, as I by these presents do declare, each and every one of the persons included in these fifteen families, their children, and legitimate descendants, to be noblemen (hijos dalgo de solar conocido), and as such they shall be considered, and accorded all the honors and prerogatives, enjoyed by all landed noblemen and knights of the kingdoms of Castile according to the customs (fueros) and laws of Spain, with which His Majesty has been pleased to honor them. The proper dispatches bearing this declaration shall be issued to them by my superior office for their use whenever they shall request them. This dispatch shall be kept in the archives of the superior government council. The governor shall let them know the contents thereof, and he shall give them any official copies (testimonies) of it they may request.

Mexico City, November 28, 1730.

El Marquis de Casa Fuerte
By order of His Excellency,
Antonio de Aviles (witness)

Our Family
From Rodriguez to Nava

Salvador Rodriguez was born in 1688 on the island of Tenerife in the Canary Island chain, a Spanish archipelago of seven islands off the coast of northern Saharan Africa. Salvador's parents were Francisco Rodriguez, also of Tenerife, and Isabela Delos Reyes, of the island of Lanzarote, also in the Canary Islands chain. Salvador was described as having an athletic build, green eyes, and a broad face, with a dark complexion, graying black hair, and a thick beard. In the Canary Islands, he made his living as a cheese maker.

Salvador married the former Maria Perez Cabrera, also born in 1688, on Lanzarote, to parents, Domingo Cabrera and Maria Perez. Maria Perez Cabrera was described as attractive, with a long face and thin nose. She had a dark complexion with light-gray eyes and black hair. The couple married young and lived on the island of Lanzarote.

By 1715, the couple had a son, Patricio Rodriguez. Patricio was fifteen when the family left on their journey to New Spain. He was described as being of medium height, slender build, with a thin face, a dark complexion, and light-brown eyes with chestnut-colored hair.

In 1741, Patricio married Josefa Granado. Josefa was a member of the fourteenth registered Canary Island family who also journeyed from Lanzarote to their new home in New Spain. Patricio was killed on August 9, 1748, by Apache warriors during the campaigns of Pedro de Rabago y Teran against frontier Indian incursions. Josefa never remarried.

Josefa Granado was born Josefa Rodriguez Granadillo, in 1720, the daughter of Juan Rodriguez Granadillo and Maria Rodriguez-Provayna, on the island of Lanzarote. She was about ten years old when her family began the journey to New Spain. She was described as having a full face with a reddish flat nose and chestnut hair. Her father, Juan, died shortly after arriving at Vera Cruz on May 5, 1730. Tropical fever had been rampant throughout the area, and several people had been afflicted and perished, including another fellow *Isleño* Lucas Delgado, who died shortly after Juan. Both men were buried in Vera Cruz. Josefa's mother, also known as María Robaina de Bethéncourt, her maiden name, or simply María Granado, passed away on January 26, 1779, in La Villa de San Fernando de Béxar.

Josefa herself died on August 5, 1796, also in La Villa de San Fernando de Béxar. Patricio and Josefa had four children before his death. They were María Expectacia, Brigida Tomasa, Patricio Antonio, and Salvador II. His oldest was a daughter, Josefa Rosalia, born sometime between 1731 and 1736. It is possible that her mother was not Josefa Granado; nevertheless, she was raised by her.

Josefa Rosalia, called by her middle name Rosalia, was married three times during her life. The first was in 1752 to Jose de Castro, the great-grandson of Juan de Castro, one of the original soldiers of the 1716 Ramon expedition to the area.[34]

Rosalia's second marriage was in 1773 to Blas Maldonado from the Punta de Lampasos, an outpost of Nuevo León built for defense against the natives of the North. Her third marriage was in 1775 to Juan Jose Sánches, a soldier.

María Expectacia was born sometime between 1741 and 1745. She married Domingo Castelo on June 2, 1760. Domingo was from the presidio of San Luis de las Amarillas and was the son of Domingo and the former Antonia Nuñez. He was born around 1725–1745, in Lugo, a city in the northwestern region of Spain called Galicia. The couple had one daughter, María Trinidad, born 1763. He died on September 22, 1766. Maria then married Manuel Jose Salinas, born in 1722, in Rio Grande, in Coahuila, New Spain.[35]

Brigida Tomasa was born in 1746, but it is unknown if she ever married. Young Patricio Antonio Rodriguez was born on November

22, 1748. He married Ana María de la Fuente on April 3, 1780. The couple bought a lot of land on Calle Real from Juan Manuel Ruiz in the summer of 1782. In 1796, he then acquired the property of his sister, Rosalia, part of his parents' land holdings east of those belonging to Salvador Rodriguez.

The youngest son of Patricio and Josefa was Salvador Rodriguez II. He was born in La Villa de San Fernando de Béxar in 1749. Salvador II married Maria Gertrudis de la Pena. The couple had six children: José Ignacio, José Manuel, Jose Francisco, Maria Zaragoza, Mariana, Maria Antonia, and Mauricia. His first wife having died on October 6, 1782, Salvador II married Maria Luisa Guerrero in 1786; she was the daughter of Mathias Guerrero and Luisa Angulo. Maria Luisa was born January 12, 1748. With his second wife, Salvador II had two children: José Maria and Maria Josefa.

A daughter from his first marriage, Maria Antonia Rodriguez, was born in 1774. She married José Antonio Flores de Abrego, son of the famed José Joaquin Flores de Abrego, Texas rancher and patriot of the American Revolution as declared by the *Sons of the American Revolution* in 1996. José Joaquin had gathered Texas longhorn cattle and furnished them to General Bernardo de Galvez in Louisiana to help feed his five thousand troops locked in battle with British forces near Baton Rouge and Manchac.

Maria Antonia and José Antonio Flores had a total of ten children. Their daughter, Maria Gertrudis Eusevia Flores, married the famed Colonel Juan N. Seguin, a hero of the Texas Revolution and namesake of the city of Seguin. Their son, Jose Maria Victoriano, married Seguin's sister, Maria Lionides Seguin. Four of Maria Antonia's sons also fought for Texas independence alongside Colonel Seguin: Manuel Flores, Salvador Flores, Nepomuceno Flores, and Jose Flores.

Salvador II and Maria Gertrudis's son, Jose Francisco de Jesus Rodriguez, was born in 1782. He married a woman named Maria Antonia Ruiz, born 1771. Salvador II, having died in 1804, never had the chance to meet his one grandson from the couple, Crecencio Rodriguez, born in 1814. Up until at least 1860, Crecencio lived in San Antonio and Bexar County. However, sometime after that point, he moved, leaving the city his family helped to found. Crecencio moved to Pleasanton and married Rosario Robles. Their daughter, Maria de Jesus Rodriguez, known as Jesusa, was born on September 15, 1870.

Jesusa met Celso Eugenio Nava, a Mexican immigrant ten years her senior, and the couple fell in love. It is unknown if the couple met in Rockport or just decided to live there, but it was Rockport where they settled. Celso, known as Eugenio, worked his entire life at a meat market in Rockport that was owned by the Roe family. The pair had eight children over the years, six of whom were born while the couple had yet to be wed.

On October 31, 1904, Eugenio and Jesusa were married in a small ceremony at the Aransas County Courthouse. Thus began the Rodriguez-Nava family branch.

The oldest child was Juan Nava, born May 6, 1896. He died young at only twenty-one years of age on August 25, 1917. The oldest daughter, Tomasa, or Tomasita as she was known while young, was born the following year on September 17, 1897. She married Antonio Rinche, seventeen years her senior, and the couple raised a family. Antonio passed away in 1955, but Tomasa lived a long life, passing away on April 2, 1982, at the age of eighty-four.

Then came Josefa in 1898, Medarda in 1900, Virginia in 1901, Eugenio Jr. in 1903, Hortencia in 1905, and George in 1908.

Medarda, or Lola as she was known, was born June 4, 1900. She appeared different than her siblings. She was tall and light skinned, having more of a European look. It became known, though not widely, that her birth father was not Eugenio. As Jesusa and Eugenio were not married, she had seen another man at least on one occasion during those early years. Her father was a Rockport native, and his identity was generally known at the time, though his name had been lost to the years. Regardless, Lola was raised as the natural-born daughter of Eugenio.

Eugenio Jr. was born September 28, 1903, and lived as a local fisherman for all his life. He died young, on his twenty-sixth birthday, September 28, 1929, at home. His younger brother George found his body. The death certificate listed him as succumbing to consumption, which we know now as tuberculosis.

Hortencia, or Tencha, was born on June 1, 1905. In 1922, she married Gavino Tapia Garza, a truck driver. The couple had three sons—Osvaldo "Nito," born 1923; Frank, born 1931; and Joe Henry, born 1942—and three daughters—Susie, born 1925; Esther, born 1926; and Beatriz, born 1936.

George Nava, the youngest of Eugenio and Jesusa's children, was born July 17, 1908. He was married twice, the first to a woman named Francis and then, in 1945, to Helen Dominguez. Tragically, George committed suicide early in the morning on July 14, 1966. He shot himself in the temple with a .38-caliber revolver.

On February 13, 1925, the family's matriarch, Jesusa, passed away. Eugenio would never remarry and spent the rest of his life in Rockport surrounded by his children and their families. He would die tragically on January 4, 1951, having been struck by a truck while crossing Highway 35 to visit the home of his eldest daughter, Tomasa. He was ninety years old.

When her mother passed, Lola went to live with her sister, Hortencia, and her husband, Gavino Garza. She soon met an older man named Cecilio Mondragon. The pair dated, and Lola got pregnant. On February 1, 1926, Medarda gave birth to Cecilio Rodolfo Nava, named after Mondragon, though everyone called him Rudy.

Medarda got pregnant with her son shortly after moving in with her sister's family. Though she was seeing Mondragon, she was actually impregnated by her brother-in-law, Gavino Garza. Growing up, this soon became apparent to everyone else as Gavino's sons—Osvaldo, Francisco, and Henry—all looked similar in appearance to Rudy. However, since Medarda was already in a relationship with plans to marry Mondragon, it was decided to tell him the child was his.

When young Rudy was two years old, Medarda and Cecilio Mondragon got married in Aransas County. The couple and child moved to Victoria, Texas. By 1930, however, Medarda's relationship with Cecilio became strained. Eventually growing tired of Cecilio's violent outbursts, she called her father, Eugenio, to pick her up; she was leaving. Medarda moved back in with her father in Rockport.

Rudy grew up in Rockport, worked hard, and met the young Clara Munoz. After distinguished service in World War II, fighting in Europe, the young couple had six children and settled in Alice, later returning to Rockport around 1950. They raised their children, who, in turn, each built their own families, making the Nava family eventually one of the largest in Rockport.

Hortencia's family grew large, and everyone affectionately knew her as Tia Tencha. Gavino died on June 6, 1975, but Hortencia lived on until January 24, 1984, passing at the age of seventy-eight. Her older sister, Virginia, or Tia Nina, had a large family as well. She married young in 1919 to Gregorio Solis and had five sons and two daughters. Gregorio passed in 1964, but Virginia stayed with us longer, passing on September 8, 1986, at the age of eighty-five.

Medarda passed away on October 3, 1986, having been known and loved by her seven grandchildren, sixteen great-grandchildren, and, at the time, one great-great grandson, all in attendance for her memorial service. The home she lived in for over sixty years was moved, intact, to the land located directly behind the home of her son, Rudy.

Later in life, Rudy suffered heart problems and grew ill. His wife of sixty-four years, Clara, devoted her time to caring for him. However, it was Clara who passed first in 2007. Heartbroken and surrounded by family, Rudy passed the following year, joining his beloved Clara, whom Rudy had fondly nicknamed Miss Ellie, after the matriarch of the popular television series *Dallas*. After the passing of Rudy and Clara Nava, the family began to disperse, some relocating to San Antonio. However, the Navas remain a presence in the Rockport area.

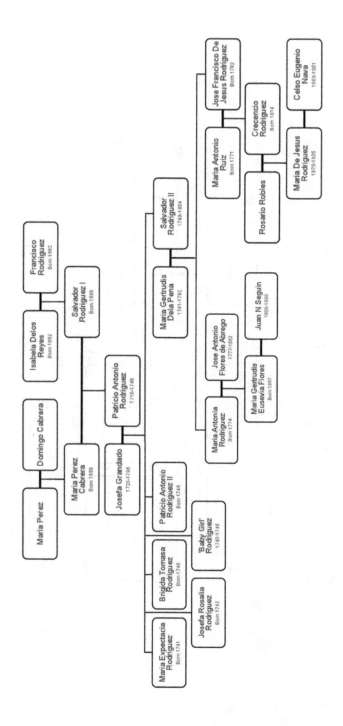

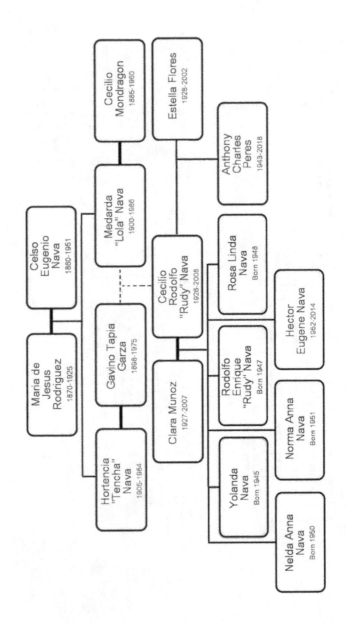

Halloween, c. 1890s, Maria de Jesus Rodriguez (1870–1925),
far right, dressed as a gypsy, with friends.

Nava home, Rockport, 1910. (*L-to-R*) George, Celso Eugenio,
Medarda, Juan, Josefa, and a neighbor.

Nava sisters, Rockport, 1912. (*L-to-R*) Hortencia, 7;
Medarda, 12; Virginia, 11; and Josefina, 14.

Medarda "Lola" Nava.

Cecilio Rodolfo "Rudy" Nava, as a young boy.

Cecilio Mondragon believed he was the father of Rudy Nava.

Clara Munoz, age 1.

Enrique Munoz, holding baby Clara, c. 1927.

Early Life in San Antonio

Before the arrival of the *Isleños*, there were roughly forty-five soldiers stationed in the Presidio de San Antonio de Béxar. About four families lived in the surrounding area, and an additional nine soldiers rotated among the area missions. The total civilian population for the unincorporated region was about two hundred people. The arrival of the *Isleños* added a further fifty-six persons to that community.

Once the *Isleños* arrived, Captain Juan Antonio Pérez de Almazán had to establish a way to keep civil order aside from the military community that already existed at the nearby presidio. On July 20, 1731, approximately five months after the *Isleños*' arrival, Captain Almazán formed the first *cabildo*, or city council. He appointed the council's first members, selecting the eldest and most respected of the *Isleños*, Don Juan Leal Goraz, as the first *regidor*, or councilman. This appointment made sense as Don Juan had been the leader of the *Isleños* throughout their journey from the Canary Islands. Captain Almazán selected the rest of the council: Juan Curbelo, second *regidor*; Antonio Santos, third *regidor*; Salvador Rodríguez, fourth *regidor*; Manuel de Niz, fifth *regidor*, and Juan Leal Jr., sixth *regidor*. Each *regidor* would be responsible for overseeing a different aspect of villa business. Curbelo would be in charge of the new jail to be constructed. Santos was responsible for official weights and measures. Rodríguez would supervise all warehouses and public buildings. Manuel de Niz would be responsible for any unclaimed property, while Juan Leal Jr. would take over no other extra duties other than being a voting member of the *cabildo*.

In addition to those *regidors*, Captain Almazán needed others to assist in civic oversight and law enforcement for the now-growing community. He appointed Vicente Álvarez Travieso to be the first *alguacil mayor*, or sheriff. He also appointed Antonio Rodríguez to the position of *mayordomo de los propios*, or public lands administrator. Back in the Canary Islands, Antonio Rodríguez was a skilled irrigator. Here he would be responsible again for the irrigation system as well as the overall cleanliness of the villa. The position would also be responsible for collecting debts and revenues, basically acting as city attorney. Captain Almazán, under the authority of the governor, made these all life appointments.

On August 1, 1731, Captain Almazán administered the oath of office to each of the newly appointed villa officials. Each swore to be loyal and to carry out the responsibilities of their respective offices faithfully. The *cabildo's* first task was to elect two *alcades*, mayors, amounting to the first civil election in Texas. The eight voting members unanimously voted Don Juan Leal Goraz to be the first *alcalde*. A second ballot was called, and Don Salvador Rodríguez was elected the second *alcalde*.

The next order of business was what to call their new villa. The *cabildo* debated back and forth, but the whole conversation was moot when Captain Almazán notified them that the viceroy had already chosen a name: San Fernando de Béxar (or Bexar), so named to honor the king's son, Crown Prince Fernando. So it was done. The first organized civil government in Texas was born.[36]

Now that the *Isleños* were here, they had to integrate with those that were already living in the area. One way to foster community and bring people together is through food. According to some historians, the food of the *Isleños* heavily influenced what we now know nationally as Tex-Mex. It was the *Isleños* that introduced cilantro, cumin, and possibly even some chili peppers into Texas colonial cooking. When combined with local ingredients like beef, pecans, and pinto beans, with the added smoked flavor of mesquite wood-fueled cooking, Tex-Mex arose.

The *Isleños* brought with them recipes for mojo sauce, a must-have condiment for most dishes. Mojo sauce came in two varieties, *verde* and *rojo*. *Mojo verde*, or Canarian green sauce, is a delicious cilantro-infused sauce, thick in consistency, not creamy, with garlic, oil, and cumin. *Mojo rojo* is red and made with oil, vinegar, chili, garlic, cumin, and paprika. Today, you can find many different versions of this sauce with no two recipes alike. Sound familiar? These are directly related to the *salsa verde* and *salsa rojo* that just about every Tex-Mex restaurant brings out to your table with chips. The sauces have made their way around the world but originated in the Canary Islands.

Additionally, the *Isleños* loved cheese. With no experience as ranchers and practically no cattle in the Canary Islands, Canarian *queso*, or cheese, was primarily made from goats. Also known as *queso de cabra*, this creamy goat cheese can be enjoyed alone or with a little added garlic and served with bread as *almogrote*, similar to Tex-Mex *queso* and chips.

There's also a delicious rabbit stew with tomatoes, called *conejo al salmorejo*, or there's *sancocho*, another meat-and-vegetable stew, sometimes made with boiled sea bass and served with potatoes and mojo sauce. Any way you serve it, *Isleños* brought with them a cuisine that has endured and evolved, adding Native American influences, and traces of it all can still be found in authentic Tex-Mex.[37]

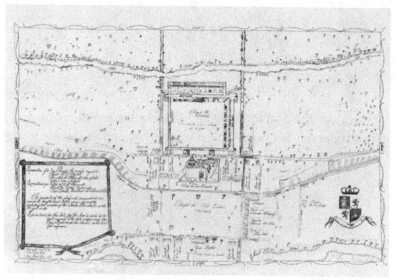

Plazas of San Antonio, circa 1778 (undated compilation by John Ogden Leal, UTSA Special Libraries Collection).[38]

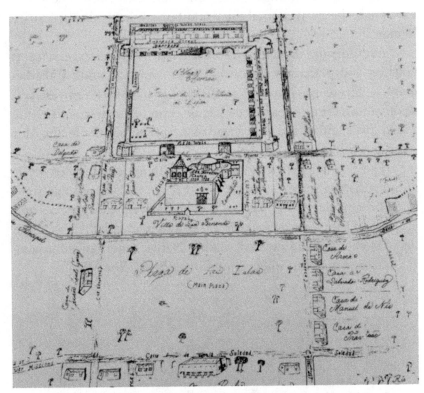

Close-up of the San Antonio Plaza, 1778: The homestead of Salvador
Rodriguez is on the north side of the plaza on what is now Commerce Street.
The home of Juan Leal Goraz is on the opposite side, on what is
now Dolorosa Street. Both are shown to be east of Soledad,
near the San Fernando Cathedral.[39]

Goraz v. Rodriguez[40]

Now that the newly arrived Canary Islanders had established La Villa de San Fernando, the king expressed his gratitude. Each colonist and their heirs were granted, in perpetuity, the noble title of *Hidalgo*. As is typical with many when given a little privilege, some of these new landowning noblemen developed a degree of self-importance, especially towards the area's established populace. Of these few, senior *Isleño* Juan Leal Goraz was considered by some to be not very tolerant or fair-minded, not only by his fellow colonists but also by some members of the clergy and military.

In 1731, when Juan Leal Goraz was appointed first *regidor* of the town council and later elected *alcalde*, his arrogance was said to have grown commensurately. As a result, by 1733, he was replaced as mayor by Antonio de los Santos. Though few can claim Goraz was easy to navigate, he was well respected. His few years as the first mayor were successful, and his clashes with his fellow *Isleños* were relatively minor.

One of the *Isleños* Goraz had an issue with was Vicente Álvarez Travieso. Travieso would later be the first *Alguacil Mayor*, or sheriff, of La Villa de San Fernando. During their journey, while passing through San Luis Potosí, Goraz issued a loan to Travieso. When the group arrived in Coahuila, Goraz tried to collect. He was adamant that the deadline for repayment had passed and demanded payment in full. While on the arduous journey across the territory, there was little opportunity for Travieso to make any money for which to repay the loan. Goraz even tried to bring the issue before the courts in Coahuila. This would prove to be just one of many instances of litigious behavior on the part of Goraz.

Later, when parcels of land were distributed to the *Isleños*, Juan Leal Goraz chose last. In doing so, he expectedly received the least favorable lot. This began a series of legal battles and claims from about 1732 to 1735, which Goraz would take up against other *Isleño* families, like the Curvelos, the Padróns, the Santoses, and the Traviesos. One such legal battle that Goraz initiated was against the family of his close friend and fellow senior *Isleño*, Salvador Rodriguez.

Salvador Rodriguez was born sometime in 1688 and was already in his early forties when he made the journey over from the Canary Islands. When Juan Leal Goraz was unanimously elected *alcalde*, Rodriguez was elected as second *alcalde*, akin to a comayor, an influential and respected position. Unfortunately, Rodriguez died sometime around 1734, leaving his widow, María Perez Cabrera, and son, Patricio Rodriguez to care for their land and homestead. María was about forty-six at this time, while Patricio was about nineteen. Patricio was possibly already the single father of a young daughter, Josefa Rosalia Rodriguez, probably born sometime after 1731 to an unknown mother. Tending to the ranch and supporting the family were daunting tasks for anyone, much more so for a new widow, son, and young granddaughter.

On August 29, 1734, Juan Leal Goraz went before Don Manuel de Sandoval, captain general and governor of the province. Goraz, still a senior *regidor* with the *cabildo*, filed a formal charge with the provincial governor. The criminal complaint was against young Patricio Rodriguez. Don Juan Leal affirmed that earlier that very same day, while in his home, Patricio showed up and proceeded to assault him verbally. Patricio's father, the late Don Salvador, owed Don Juan Leal a small sum of money. He requested that young Patricio assume his father's debt and pay him the money owed. At first, Patricio was expectedly shocked at the request, and after Don Juan Leal left, he grew angry at the seemingly unreasonable demand. Patricio reportedly visited the Goraz home and complained that the demand was unjust and unreasonable. He allegedly made several rude comments toward Don Juan Leal. Don Juan Leal further attested that Patricio pulled a knife, which he had always carried in his belt. He allegedly called Don Juan Leal a *Morisco,* a term for *Isleño* descendants of Muslim Moors, in this case, used with derogatory connotations.[41]

Don Juan Leal's eldest son, Juan Leal, known as *El Mozo*, tried to intercede on his father's behalf. He implored Patricio to leave their property in peace and to be respectful when talking to a man of Don Juan Leal's years. Patricio purportedly replied that he could "go to hell" and that he shouldn't stand up for a man such as his father. Nonetheless, Patricio did leave and return to his home, retrieving a carbine rifle. Don Juan Leal stated that he then returned, along with his mother, María. Seeing the gun and believing the visibly angry Patricio might do something foolish, Don Juan Leal remained inside. Patricio called out that "if anyone wanted to collect the debt, he could come outside," again referring to Don Juan Leal and his family as *Moriscos*. Patricio and his mother eventually left and returned home. It is possible that María came along to beseech Don Juan Leal and to temper the anger of young Patricio, ensuring he did nothing rash.

Once they left, Don Juan Leal seethed with anger, feeling the public spectacle harmed his good name and reputation. It was at that time, he stated, that he chose to file a formal complaint with the provincial office. The governor heard the complaint and reviewed the allegation. Since this was a criminal charge, he had little choice but to sign the decree that Patricio Rodriguez be taken into custody pending the outcome of the investigation. This decree directed the current *alcalde*, Don Manuel de Niz to issue orders for Patricio's apprehension. Manuel de Niz complied with the directive and sent Asencio del Raso to locate Patricio, whom he immediately found in his home. He was arrested and taken to the guardroom until the governor could rule on the criminal complaint.

On September 6, 1734, Governor Sandoval held a formal hearing on the complaint. He called María, Patricio's mother, to give testimony. She swore out a petition acknowledging Don Juan Leal's complaint against her son. However, she further claimed that Patricio, being held in custody, was causing undue hardship on her. María requested "in all humility before the great beneficence of your lordship, to take pity on a poor helpless widow." She asked that the governor order Don Juan Leal to come forth and rescind his complaint. She further explained that Don Juan Leal had already agreed to do so verbally to Don Joseph de la Garza y Arellano, the vicar priest and ecclesiastical judge. It seemed that since the incident, Don Juan Leal's anger had receded, and he believed that Patricio's incarceration for the past eight days should be considered punishment enough for his impulsive behavior.

María pleaded to the governor to, therefore, order her son's release. As Patricio was her only son, he was the only one to help "nourish and protect me, at his own expense." Additionally, she cried that without Patricio to tend to the crops, they are in danger of being lost altogether, "consequently we shall all perish because we have no recourse except the patronage and protection of your Lordship."

The governor was not a heartless man. He reviewed María's petition but found it to be out of order. He understood that Patricio's incarceration was causing an undue hardship upon the widow due to the delays of harvesting the crops. He stated that he further understood how wholly dependent she was upon her son. Though he did rule against María's petition, he acknowledged that any further delay in the proceedings could cause the family's entire crop to be lost. However, the governor was scheduled to hold the *residencia* hearing concerning the former provincial governor, General Don Juan Antonio de Bustillo y Zavallos (Ceballos). He also had other vital petitions to hear, which caused all other nonserious matters to be postponed, including the case of Patricio Rodriguez. However, realizing the hardship on the widow and in the service of justice, Governor Sandoval ordered that if a reliable person "would be responsible for the person of Patricio Rodriguez, promising to produce him upon demand, to satisfy the costs which may be incurred by him, and making written bond to that effect, the said Patricio Rodriguez shall be released." In the presence of the full municipal council, the governor signed this order.

That same day, upon receiving the governor's order, the *alcalde* himself, Don Manuel de Niz, vowed that he would give "bond for, and receive into his custody, as a prisoner on parole, Patricio Rodriguez." He affirmed that he would be responsible for ensuring that Patricio would appear before the court as ordered. He further maintained that he would be responsible for payment of any court costs that may be incurred from the charges against Patricio.

It is reported that Don Manuel did not actually sign the court's certification because he did not know how. Witnesses who confirmed the certification included Don Joseph Bueno de Roxas, Domingo de Hoyos, and Don Fermin de Ivisicu. All three affirmed Don Manuel's statement in the presence of the governor and the secretary of the municipal council, Francisco Joseph de Arocha.[42]

Early the following day, on September 7, 1734, in light of the governor's order, Francisco Joseph de Arocha and Don Manuel made their way to the guardroom where Patricio was being held. Corporal Andres Hernandez reviewed the order and certification and promptly retrieved Patricio. Patricio Rodriguez was released into the custody of Don Manuel.

Eventually, as the story is told, Patricio Rodriguez was found guilty of the charges against him, not that he ever refuted them. He spent several months imprisoned locally until finally the local *curate*[43] could secure Patricio's release.[44]

Often during this first decade or so of life in their new home, numerous complaints and petitions were filed with the governor's office, usually to collect on bills of credit. The ease upon which the settlers engaged in lawsuits upon one another became a fixture of the early days of San Fernando. One of the most serious involved Don Juan Leal filing a complaint, in 1734, against a fellow *Isleño*, accusing him of making a statement that he would not obey the royal commands. As a consequence of Don Juan Leal's testimony, this *Isleño* spent some time imprisoned in the municipal guardhouse. At least, the tendency to take the law into one's own hands was rare, and most seemed perfectly willing to live under the rule of law.[45]

In the end, Don Juan Leal Goraz died around 1742, surrounded by his family in the municipality he helped found. Interestingly enough, Patricio Rodriguez was elected *alcalde* that same year, himself passing away just six short years later.

Milam Park in San Antonio, adjacent to the old "Campo Santo," burial
spot for many of the original Canary Islanders, including Salvador
Rodriguez I. The park also features a tribute to the alcaldes and mayors of
San Antonio, including Patricio Rodriguez I and Salvador Rodriguez II.

Patricio Rodriguez I served as alcalde of San Antonio in 1742.
His son, Salvador Rodriguez II, served in 1785 and 1796.

Last Will and Testament of Salvador Rodriguez II (1749–1804)

(Transcription of the original 1804 will of Salvador Rodriguez II, son of Patricio Rodriguez I. The original is located in the archives of the University of Texas at Austin)[46]

[HISPANIAR REX.	SELLO TERCERO, DOS REA
CAROLUS—IV—D.G.]	LES, AÑOS DE MIL OCHO
	CIENTOS QUATRO, Y OCHO
	CIENTOS CINCO

En el nombre (de)la Sma Trinidad Padre, Hijo, y Espiritu Santo tres personas divinas, y un solo Dios verdadero. Amen.

Sepan los que me vieren como Io. D. Salvador Rodrigues originario, y vecino (de) una Villa (de)San Fernando y Preso. (de)S. Antonio de Vejar orando grabeme enfermo (de) accidente que dios en el ha sido servido embiarme; pero por su misericordia infinita en mi entero Juicio, memoria y entendimiento natural, creyendo, como firmemente creo todos los Articulos, y misterios de nuestra Sta Fee Catolica; en la qual profeso vivir y morir; y temiendo como es natural, que llegada la incierta ho re (de)la muerte que al fin se me hade llegar; para que esta me halle enterame prevenido, hago, ordeno, y establesco mi testamento y ulti-ma voluntad en laforma siguiente.

1 Primerame encomiendo mi alma a Dios N.S. que la Crio, y redimio con supreciosisima sangre, y mi cuerpo lo mando de la tierra (de) que fue formado

2a Ite declaro que quando Dios sea servido sacarme (de) esta vida para la otra, mi cuerpo sea sepultado en la Parroquia (de)esta

41

Villa, y mi cuerpo amortajado con la mortaja que se encontrare; dejan-do a determinacion de mi Alvacea y herederos la disposision (de)l entierro; a lo quales encargo toda moderacion en él, y lo declaro para que conste

3a Ite. declaro haber sido casado enprimeras nupcias conda Maria Gertrudis (de)la Peña de cuyo Matrimonio hubo seis hijos que ex isten; llamados José Ig.o José Manuel, Jose Fran.co Maria Zaragoza, Mariana, y María Antonía, y Mauricía que despues despues de casada murio sin sucesion, y en segundas nupcias soy acutalme casado con d.a Maria Luisa Guerrero, (de) cuyo matrimonio existen dos hijos que por sucesion leg. ma he tenido; llamado Jose Maria y Maria Josefa declarolo para que conste.

4a Ite. Mando á cada una (de) las mandas forzosas, un rl entre-gandolo á qn. Las colectare y lo declare para que conste

5a Ite. Declare por mis bienes muebles las reces que se encuen-tren en el Rancho dela Candelaria con mi Fierro y señal. Siete potranquias y un caballo que tambien permanecen en dho Rancho son pertencecientes a mi hijo José Maria por haberlas adquiri-do con su inteligencia y solicitud, nueve caballos de my servo delos quales se ex cluira un tordillito que es tambien perte-neciente á mi dho hijo José Ma. por que haberlo adquirido por mercid, ocho yuntas de [ilegible] oilles milusos tres toros 60 mulas de los quales uno pert-enece a mi hijo Igo. cinco carretas nuevas, tres rejas viejas, dos achas, dos asadones gres. y otro chico, dos Escoplos, una asuda, una olla de acero un caso Rancho y un metate, que estan en dho, pertenecen a mi caporal Conrazon por haberlo traido a mi poder declarolo para que conste.

6a Ite. declaro tener en el referido Rancho sembradas las dos labores (de)l pan, y plasita, y quatro alm.s (de)sembradura en la labor vieja; pues aunque hay otro sembrador alli mismo no tiene parte en ello mas de mi hijo Igo. el pedaso que le tengo señalado, y el muchacho pe hnojalera en dos almudes en sembradura que le asigna, declarolo para q. conste.

7a Ite. declaro por mis dhos bienes ocho horas (de)agua, con las tierra (de) laborio correspondientes, citras en la labor (de)abajo de este Pres (de)las quales quatro horas y media con sus tierras hube

(de) mis difuntos Padres, y los restantes por compra q. hise á mi
herma. Rosalia (de)q. no tengo documento, una casa fabricada (de)
adove y techa da (de) tela, que se compone como (de) catorce varas
en la qual solo hube por herencia de mis padres laparte q. me corre-
spondió, y lo proveniente es (de)la parte que compre á mi hermana
Egipciaca, durante mi primera muger por lo que los hijos (de) este
matrimonio Son acredores á la parte materna que alli parece, dos
partes (de)la fabrica material (de)la casa (de) mi cuñado Jn. Salvador
Dias la una q. me correspondio (de) mis padres y la otra que compre
á mi dha hemana Egipciaca, ocho varas (de) tierra y dies (de)fondo
contiguas á la dha casa compradas durante mi primer matrimonio,
las que poseo sin documto. alguno no obstante haber sido leg. ma la
compra declarolo para que consta.

8a Ite. declaro por mis dhos bienes la casa que actualme. poseo
fabricada deterrado; la qual compre durante mi seg.do matrimonio
con mi solicitud y la (de) mi actual mu ger sin tocar (de)los bienes
muebles ni raises q. poseo dha casa tiene su correspondiente fondo al
Arroyo, declarolo para que consta.

9a Ite. declaro que al mismo tpo que compré la casa anteri-
or(ente) di dos cientos pesos al capitan retirado D. José Menchaca,
a cuenta (de) otra casa que trato (de) venderme, y como hsta ahora
no lo ha verificado, y si ofrecido bolverme la ex presada cantidad
lo declaro para constancia, como tambien el que dhos doscientos
p. fueron adquiridos (de)l mismo modo que los 550 referidos en la
clausula anterior y lo declaro

10 Ite. declaro deverme á d Benito (de) Oicton lo que conste
por sus libros a D. Xavier Palan cinquenta y quatro p. para el tpo
que dice la obligacion, á la Viuda (de)l difunto D. Luis Menchaca lo
que conste por sus apuntes, al Sargento Andres (de)l Valle treinta p.
declarolo para q. conste.

11 Ite. declaro deverme Jn Antonio Safore dose p. ō un puerta
para la que debe poner las maderas necesarias declarolo para q. conste

12 Ite. declaro deber á mi Enterrado José Ernandes dos toritos
(de)los de tres años; y doce misas á beneficio (de)l alma (de)l difunto
Fray José Ma. Salas, declarolo para q. conste

13 Ite. declaro que todos los tramos al servicio dedentro decasa son pertenecientes a mi actual Esposa por haberlos traido á mi poder declarolo para que conste.

14 Ite. declaro tener una Esclava Mulata llamada Maria Manuela la que compre durante mi actual muger en cantidad decien p. y lo declaro para que conste.

15 Ite. declaro que quando me case con la actual muger traxe a supoder veinte y dos cabesas (de)ganado mayor, y por haberse procreado estas el numero (de) reses que hoy existente para no inferir agravio á unos ni otros herederos, ni á mi Esposa por rason (de)las gananciales que deben corresponderle es mi voluntad q. (de)l referido numero de reses se hagan tres partes iguales, y se ad judiquen la una á los hijos de mi primer matrimonio solo la otra á los del primero y segundo, y la otra á mi Qda Esposa por sus gananciales, declarolo para que conste.

16 Ite. declaro que mando (de)lafacultad que el Dio me permite para poder libreme. disponer (de)l tercio y quinto (de) mis bienes, dejo á mi hijo Igo. por via (de) mejora una carreta y otra Suma de muebles á mi hijo José Man. otra carreta y otra Suma de muebles, y á mi hijo José Ma. y su madre dos carretas y dos Sumas muebles, siendo estos ultimos preferidos en la eleccion (de)los muebles, al dho mi hijo José Ma. tambien es mi voluntad dejarlo mejorado con un caballo colorado (de)camino q. está en el sinado, declarolo para q. conste.

17 Ite. declaro que á la susodha mi muger hiso gracia de una becerri ta acabada (de) naser la que exis y se conserva hta el dia pero logicame. corresponde á ella, también á mis hijos José Ma y Ma Josefa señalé a cada uno una ternerita con las quales han procurado el primero cinco cabesas, y la segunda dos, declarolo para q. conste.

18 Ite. declaro que es mi voluntad que la actual casa demi morada n[ilegible] [ilegible]mse en el todo (de)l cuerpo (de)los bienes, sino que sesepare para mi dha Esposa y sus dos hijos respecto á tener aquella la mitad (de) dha casa y los otros cada uno lasuya; y por qué á los hijos (de) mi primer matrimonio es mui corta la parte que en ella les puede corresponder les encargo que como hijos obedientes acudan á tomarla o que seles remplase con lo que á los dos hijos

(de)l seg.do matrimonio les corresponda en la otra casa expresada en la clausula septima (de) esta disposicion; y si una no alcansare á recompensarles su importe, mi dha actual muger selas pagará (de)lo que á ella secorresponda; e igualme. es mi ultima voluntad; y asi lo suplico á los expresados mis hijos que la labor del Rancho nombrada la plasota y la (de)l paso por es tár yá corriente, i immediata á la vivienda (de) dho Rancho quede para quela Qra mi actual muger, y sus dos hijos gozen (de)su beneficis imos viva, declarolo para que conste.

19 Ite. declaro por mis dhos bienes una Escopeta la qual dejo asignada para mi hijo José María y lo declaro para q. conste

20 Ite. declaro quepamayor niveliga y evitar confusion acerca (de)lo expresado en la clausula 18 digo que [ilegible] (de)que en la medida q. corres pondan en dha casa á mi actual Esposa tengan alguna parte los herederos, selos recompensará ella misma con su propio dinero, ó inteligencias para que la dejen vivr quieta y pacificamente en ella, por no ser absoluta para determinar (de)la parte que en la otra casa, y solar pertenecen á sus dos hijos declaro pa. que conste.

21 Ite. mando que verificado mi fallecimto. se saque (de) mis dhos bienes el importe (de) un novenario de misas á beneficio (de) mi alma y lo declaro para q. consta.

22 Ite. declaro que por ser el mayor (de)todos mis hijos José Igo. es mi voluntad, que este quede entendiendo en el manejo y cuidado (de)todos los bienes (de) Rancho y Lavor hasta que se cumpla todo lo dispuesto en esta mi ultima voluntad pagandole por su trabajo siempre que tenga buen desempeño en este encargo, con los mismos frutos que coseche, lo que se concidere Justo, declaro para que conste.

23 Ite. declaro que la Laborcita vieja (de) dho Rancho que actualme tiene sembrada mi dho hijo Ig. selo quede para sugose co-mo por via (de) mejora declarolo pa. q conste.

24 Ite. declaro que sin embargo (de) haber dispuesto en este mi testam.to (de)las tierras (de) dho Rancho estas las he estado posiyando de buena fee cuyo dño es el q. tengo adquirido hta el dia y lo declaro para q. conste

25 Ite. declaro que si cuando parecieren algunas vestias (de) mi fierro (de)las q. tengo perdidas las recoja mi hijo José Maria para su

uso dejendolo proferido en el di (de)l fierro y señal por ser el menor (de)todos y lo declaro para que conste.

26 Ite. declaro que mi hija Mauricia, aunque murio (de)parto y lapobre sobrevivio despues (de)su muerte algunos dias, (de)lo que acaso pueda corresponderle se rebajará el costo (de)l entierro (de) ella por haberlo sopor-tado de ella mis bienes, y mi hija Mariana el costo (de)l entierro (de)la criatura á mi hija Mariana por haberlo costeado ella

Ite. cumplido y pagado con mi testamento, mandas y (de)mas dispuesto en este mi testamento; en el remanente (de) todos mis bienes derechos y acciones instituyo y nombro por mis unicos, y uni-versales herederos á los referidos mis hijos, para que los hayan posen y dis-fruten con la vendicion (de) Dios y la mia instruyendo por Alvaceas y ejecutores (de) este mi testam.to en mi primer lugar á mi esposa D.a Ma. Luisa Guerrero y en segundo á mi hijo José Ignacio Rodrigues á quienes doy poder y facultad para q. librem.e puedan hacer (de) mis bienes lo que jusguen conveniente hasta desempeñar las respectivas obligaciones (de)su encargo. Yo D. Tomas (de) Arocha Alc.e ordi-nario de primer voto doy fee conocer al testador y haber presenciado esta Su ultima voluntad que ha echo al parecer en su[illegible] Juicio, memoria y natural acuerdo presentes D. Manuel Flores, D. Ignacio Lucero y D. Felis Ruiz como testig. instrumentales, llamados y roga-dos por el tes-y vecinos tador, siendo todos originarios, (de) esta Villa (d)S. Ferñdo y Pres (de) Bejar dondes es fecha á ocho de Abril (de) mil ochocientos quatro años Doy fee - enmendado- Mauricia endos partes—entre renglones y vecinos – todo Vale--

[Firma: Thomas de Arocha
[Firma: Salvador Rodrigues]

[Firma: Jose Ant.o Saucedo] [Firma:Agustin Ruiz]

[HISPANIAR REX. CAROLUS—IV—D.G.]

SELLO TERCERO, DOS les, AÑOS DE MIL OCHO CIENTOS QUATRO, Y OCHO CIENTOS CINCO

Translation of the Last Will and Testament of Salvador Rodriguez II (1749–1804)[47]

KING OF SPAIN	THIRD SEAL, TWO REALES
CAROLUS-IV	YEARS FROM ONE THOUSAND
THANKS BE TO GOD	EIGHT HUNDRED FOUR TO EIGHT
	HUNDRED FIVE

In the name of the Holy Trinity—Father, Son, and Holy Spirit—three divine persons and one and only true God. Amen.

Let it be known to those who know me as D. Salvador Rodrigues native, and neighbor of Villa San Fernando and Presidio San Antonio de Vejar, that praying, seriously ill due to an accident that God has sent me; but by his infinite mercy in my right mind, memory and natural consciousness, believing, as I firmly believe in all the Articles [of faith], and mysteries of our Holy Catholic Faith; in which I profess to live and die; being afraid as it is natural, that once the unforeseeable time of death arrives which at the end must come to me; and for it to find me fully prepared, I make, order, and establish my will and last wishes in the following manner.

1st Firstly, I entrust my soul to our God who created it, and redeemed it with his precious blood, and sent my body from the soil from which it was created.

2nd Item I declare that whenever it pleases God to take me from this life to the other, may my body be buried in the Parish of this Town, and may my body be shrouded with the shroud that may be found; leaving it to the consideration of my executor and heirs the arrangement of the burial; and to them I entrust [to exercise] restrain on it, and I declare it so that it is documented.

3rd Item I declare having been married on my first marriage to Mrs. Maria Gertrudis (de)la Peña from which marriage six children were born and they exist; named José Ignacio José Manuel, Jose Francisco Maria Zaragoza, Mariana, and Maria Antonia, and Mauricia who after being married, died leaving no succession, and that I am currently married on my second marriage with Mrs. Maria Luisa Guerrero, from which marriage two children exist and that through legitimate succession I have had; names José Maria y Maria Josefa. I declare it so that it is documented.

4th Item I bequeath a real to each of my mandatory inheritors, giving it to whoever collects them [inheritance taxes], and I declare it so that is documented.

5th Item I declare as my belongings the livestock that is found in Rancho de la Candelaria, branded with my mark: seven fillies, and a horse that also is kept in the aforementioned Ranch they also belong to my son José Maria since he obtained them through his intelligence and diligence, nine horses that serve me of which shall also be excluded a dapple-grey horse that also belongs to my aforementioned son, José Maria, since he acquired it as a gift, eight pairs of 50 multipurpose yoking animals[48], three bulls, 60 mules of which one belongs to my son Ignacio, five new carts,[49] three old plowshares, two axes, two big hoes and a small one, two chisels, one waterwheel, one steel pot, one pot and a grinding stone, all of which is found in the aforementioned Ranch, they belong to my foreman since he brought it to my possession. I declare it so that it is documented.

6th Item I declare that in the aforementioned Ranch I have sowed the two cereal/grain fields, and "la plasita,"[50] and four fields "almudes[51] de sembradura" in the old fields; since even though there are other cultivated fields in that same place, he [my son] does not have any share on it. [The only share] my son Ignacio [has,] is the portion that I have designated for him, and the young man will [illegible] in the two sowing "almudes" that are assigned to him. I declare it so that it is documented.

7th Item I declare as my aforementioned belongings eight hours of water, with the corresponding working fields, situated in the fields located downstream of this Presidio, of which four and a half hours along with its fields I obtained from my deceased parents, and the remaining ones [I obtained] through a purchase I made from my sister Rosalia, for which I have no document; a house made of adobe with cloth roof, that is comprised of fourteen "varas"[52] which I only inherited from my parents the part that corresponded to me, and the rest is from the part I bought from my sister Egipciaca, during the time I was with my first wife and therefore, the children from this marriage are deserving of the maternal part that is stipulated; two parts of the house belonging to Juan Salvador Dias, my brother in law, one part of which I inherited from my parents, and the other part I bought from my aforementioned sister, Egipciaca, a lot of eight "varas" and ten [varas] deep located next to the aforementioned house, bought during my first marriage, which I own with no document [to prove it] even though the purchase was legitimate. I declare it so that it is documented.

8th Item I declare as part of my aforementioned belongings the house that I currently own, made out of stucco/dirt; which I bought during my second marriage through my diligence and that of my current wife without making use of any belongings nor real state that I own. The aforementioned house has the river on the back. I declare it so that it is documented.

9th Item I declare that at the same time that I bought the aforementioned house I gave two hundred pesos to retired Capitan Don José Menchaca, to pay for another house that he tried to sell me, and because up until now he hasn't verified it, and he has however offered to return said sum. I declare it so that it is documented. [I] also [declare] that the said two hundred pesos were acquired through the same means as the 550 denoted on the previous clause and I declare it.

10th Item I declare that I owe to Benito de Oicton the [amount] stated in his books to Don Xavier Palan fifty four pesos during the time that stipulates the obligation, to the Widow of the deceased D. Luis Menchaca the [amount] stated in his books, to Sergeant Andres del Valle thirty pesos. I declare it so that it is documented.

11th Item I declare that Juan Antonio Safore owes me twelve pesos or a door for which he must provide the necessary wood. I declare it so that it is documented.

12th Item I declare that I owe to my buried José Ernandes two little three-year old bulls; and twelve masses for the benefit of the soul of the deceased Fray José Maria Salas. I declare it so that it is documented.

13th Item I declare that all the space that gives service inside the house belongs to my current wife since she brought them to my domain. I declare it so that it is documented.

14th Item I declare that I have a mulatto slave by the name of Maria Manuela. I bought her during my current wife for one hundred pesos. I declare it so that it is documented.

15th Item I declare that when I married my current wife I brought into the marriage twenty-two heads of cattle. Since [the cattle] procreated, the number of cattle now in existence, to not offend neither of my heirs, nor my wife due to the share of profits that ought to be distributed, it is my will that the said number of cattle be divided in three equal parts, and that one part is solely given to the children of the first marriage, the other part to [the children] of the first and second marriage, and the third to my dear wife for her profits. I declare it so that it is documented.

16th Item I declare that with the authority that God affords me to be able to freely dispose of the third[53] and fifth[54] of my belongings, I leave to my son Ignacio, as a special bequest,[55] a cart and an amount of personal property; to my son José Manuel a cart and another amount of personal property; and to my son José Maria and his mother two carts and two amounts of personal property, these two being favored in the choice of property. It is also my will to leave as a special bequest to my son José María red horse for the road,[56] that is marked. I declare it so that it is documented.

17th Item I declare that the aforementioned wife bargained a little calf just born, which exists and still owns nowadays, therefore, by logic it belongs to her. Also to my children José María y María Josefa I have designated to each one of them a little calf from which [my son] has procured five heads, and [my daughter] two. I declare it so that it is documented.

18th Item I declare that it is my will that the house I currently live in [illegible] in the bulk of my belongings, but rather to be set aside for my aforementioned Wife and her two children, since she has half of said house and the others each have their own; and because the children of my first marriage have a very small claim [to this house] I ask that as obedient children they take it or that instead it is replaced with the part of the house stated on the seventh article of this will that corresponds to the two children of the second marriage. And if she [the daughter] does not have enough to pay the value, them my said current wife will pay from the part that corresponds to her. It is also my last will; and I beg from my said children that the fields in the Ranch known as "la plasita" and "el paso," since they are adjacent to the house of said Ranch be left for my Dear current wife, and her two children to live of its benefits. I declare it so that it is documented.

19th Item I declare as my said belongings a shotgun, which I designate for my son José María. I declare it so that it is documented.

20th Item I declare that for a more equitable [distribution] and to avoid confusion regarding what was stipulated in clause 18, I say that to the extent that is suitable in said house for my current Wife, some part be given to the heirs. She, herself will compensate them with her own money or diligence so that she is allowed to live peacefully in [the house], since there is no absolute way of determining the part that from the other house and plot correspond to her two children. I declare it so that it is documented.

21st Item I command that once my death is verified, the cost of a novena of masses [offered] for the benefit of my soul be deducted from my said belongings. And I declare it so that it is documented.

22nd Item I declare that since Jose Ignacio is the eldest from among all my children, it is my will that he understands the management and care of all of the property from the Ranch and Fields, until the time that everything that was declared in this my last will be fulfilled. As long as he performs well in this endeavor, his work will be compensated, in [a measure] deemed fair, with the same fruits [of his labor] that he reaps. I declare so that it is documented.

23rd Item I declare that the "Laborcita vieja" [little old field] of said Ranch that is currently being sown by my said son Ignacio, he keeps it for his benefit as his special bequest. I declare it so that it is documented.

24th Item I declare that even though I have disposed in this my will of the properties of said Ranch, I have owned [these properties] in good faith, and I own what I have acquired up to this day. I declare it so that it is documented.

25th Item I declare that when some of the marked animals that I have lost appear, my son José María shall collect them for his use, as I have promised him my brand and mark, since he is the youngest. I declare it so that it is documented.

26th Item I declare that [for] my daughter Mauricia, even though she died of labor [complications], and the poor thing survived her death for a few days, from what she could possibly be entitled to the expense of the funeral will be deducted, since I bore the cost [of it, and paid] with my properties; and my daughter Mariana funded the burial of the child, [and therefore, the amount that] my daughter Mariana spent herself [should be also deducted and reimbursed to her] Item. Once fulfilled and paid the promises and other arrangements from this my will; I establish and name as the residuary legatees of all my belongings and shares my said children as my only and universal heirs, so that they can own and enjoy [them] with God's blessing and mine. I instruct as keepers and executors of this my will, firstly my wife Doña María Luisa Guerrero, and secondly my son José Ignacio Rodrigues to whom I give [legal] power and authority to freely dispose of my belongings in a matter that they see fitting until they execute the respective obligations entrusted to them. I, Don. Tomas de Arocha, Alcalde ordinario de primer voto [1st vote mayor],[57] I attest to knowing the testator and to having witnessed this His last will that he has made seemingly in his right mind, recollection, and by his own accord [also] present Don Manuel Flores, Don Ignacio Lucero, and Don Felis Ruiz as instrumental witnesses, called and requested by the testator, [all of them] being natives and neighbors[58] of this Villa de San Fernando y Presidio de Bejar, where

today is April 8, 1804. I attest—amended—Mauricia in two parts—
in between the lines and "neighbors"[59]—all valid—

[Signature: Thomas de Arocha]
[Signature: Salvador Rodrigues]

[Signature: Jose Antonio Saucedo]
[Signature:Agustin Ruiz]

King of Spain	Third Seal, Two Reales
Carolus-IV	Years From One Thousand
Thanks be to God	Eight Hundred Four To
	Eight Hundred Five

Letter to Lord Governor Don
Benito Armiñán, 1814[60]

(Transcription of an original 1814 letter detailing Native American raids on the lands of early San Antonio settlers, including the lands of Salvador Rodriguez II)

A las once del día de ayer, llegué a la misión de San Juan en donde encontré tres paisanos de los fugitivos del Rancho del tío Calvillo, de los que llevé conmigo uno de ellos. Y en el paraje del Charco de Quiñones, yendo sobre la marcha encontré a Francisco Mireles y también lo llevé conmigo. Como poco antes de las oraciones de la noche pasé el Paso de la Candelaria cerca del Rancho de Salvador Rodríguez, en donde había cuatro becerros amarrados; fueron a reconocer si correspondían? allí o no y los encontraron muertos; seguí la marcha a mi destino y porción de huella por el camino y ambos lados lo que por ser de noche no se pudo decidir si era nuestra oveja. Y de noche en la Cañada del Nogal y antes de amanecer seguí la marcha, llegué a las 8 de la mañana al Rancho del Sargento Don Remigio Pérez en donde encontré ocho reses muertas y descarnadas por los indios, los maíces en un todo destrozados por los mismos de donde se advierte fueron al Rancho del tío Calvillo. Me dirigí allá y al llegar a él, salió el paisano Julián Zague? que se había escapado dentro de la labor, él declara que oyó estar cantando a dos indios toda la noche y que como al amanecer se ese día habían salido de allí que sería como 300 ?indios. Viendo que solo faltaba de los habitantes de ese rancho José Arriola pasé a buscarlo y se encontró muerto a las orillas del Río, mandé se le diera sepultura para enterrarlo bastante corrompido. En el Corral había 23 reses descarnadas y la Casa del Rancho quemada. Cortando la tierra ?se encontró la huella que pasaron el Río en el Paso de las Mujeres, para el Rancho de Arocha y según parece son tantos más de los que dice el paisano. Viendo que la tropa y paisanos era ?mayor de los 37 hombres, determiné seguirlos y ..pasar hacerme cargo de la huella que se vio en la noche, la que es vieja y no puede ser de estos. La tropa ha llegado .... cansada. Y a causa de esto determiné dar parte y aguardan orden de Vuestra en este punto: Dios Guarde a Vuestra Muchos Años.

Paso de la Candelaria

30 de Julio de 1814.

Domingo Marañón [rúbrica]
Señor Governador Don Benito Armiñán

Me gusta Responder

Letter to Lord Governor Don Benito Armiñán, 1814

(Translated)[61]

At eleven o'clock yesterday, I arrived at the San Juan Mission where I found three countrymen, all escapees of the ranch of Uncle Calvillo, of whom I took with me one of them. And in the place of Quiñones Pond, going on the march, I found Francisco Mireles and also took him with me. Just before the evening prayers, I passed the Candelaria Pass, near the ranch of Salvador Rodriguez, where there had been four calves tied. They went to see if they were still there or not and found them dead. I followed on with the march to my destination, still a quarter of a league, and I encountered some footprints along the road that we couldn't decide, as it was night, if they were from sheep. We spent the night in the Cañada del Nogal, and before dawn, I continued the march. I arrived at eight in the morning at the ranch of Sergeant Don Remigio Perez where I found eight cattle killed and ravaged by the Indians, all the maize (corn) destroyed by the same. Those that could escaped to the ranch of Uncle Calvillo. I went there, and when I arrived, my countryman Julian Zague came out, who had escaped in the fields; he declared that he heard two Indians singing all night, and that at dawn they had left with a group of around three hundred Indians. I saw that only one of the inhabitants of that ranch, José Arriola, was missing. I went in search of him, and he was found dead on the banks of the river. I commanded that he be buried quickly. In the corral, there were twenty-three fleshless cattle, and the ranch house had been burned. Checking the ground, we found footprints that led to the river in Woman's Pass towards the Arocha ranch and many others according to my countrymen. Seeing that the troop and civilian numbers were greater than thirty-seven men, I determined that we should follow the footprints, taking note that the one we saw the prior night was too old and could not have been from these. All the troops arrived, tired. And on account of this, I have determined to take part, and they await your {Lordship's} order in this issue.

God keep your {Lordship} many years,

Paso de la Candelaria

July 30, 1814

Domingo Marañón [rubric]
Lord Governor Don Benito Armiñán

The Flores Family,
Juan Seguin,
And the War for Texas Independence

One of the younger children of Salvador Rodriguez II and his first wife, Maria Gertrudis de la Peña, was Maria Antonia Rodriguez. She grew up in La Villa de San Fernando de Béxar and married José Antonio Flores de Abrego, son of the famed José Joaquin Flores de Abrego, Texas rancher and American Revolutionary patriot. The couple had a total of ten children, including daughter Maria Gertrudis Eusevia Flores. Maria Gertrudis Eusevia married Texas Revolutionary hero Colonel Juan N. Seguin, the namesake of the city of Seguin. Four of Maria Antonia's sons also fought for Texas independence alongside Seguin: Manuel, Salvador, Jose Maria, and Nepomuceno.

The oldest of the four brothers, Manuel, born Jose Manuel Nepomuceno Paublino Flores, was born in La Villa de San Fernando de Béxar in 1799. It is believed that he was already a widower when he married María Josefa Courbière in 1835. Later that same year, believing that Texian[62] and Mexican forces would eventually clash in nearby Gonzalez, a meeting was held at the Flores ranch. Stephen F. Austin had just approved a captain's commission for Juan Seguin and authorized him to organize and supply a company. The meeting was to try to recruit volunteers to join this company. Attendees were San Antonio area Mexicans, referred to as *Tejanos*, [63] who were willing to stand alongside Texas colonists against Mexican president Antonio López de Santa Anna. Manuel, and his brother, Salvador, had convinced forty-one volunteers from nearby ranches to join them. These ranchers turned soldiers were in favor of Texas independence. In nearby Gonzalez, colonists, immigrants, and Texian volunteers, all supporting the cause of democracy and condemning the oppressive regime of Santa Anna, continued to amass in anticipation of the coming conflict.

Manuel's brother, Salvador, was born around 1806 in La Villa de San Fernando de Béxar as Jose Salvador Ramon Flores. A skilled horseman and natural leader, he was appointed first lieutenant of the central Texas volunteers, commanding Company B of the Second Cavalry Regiment. While Seguin set about the task of supplying his company, Salvador was sent on a reconnaissance operation to survey the missions surround San Antonio de Béxar. On October 22, 1835, Salvador and his group of scouts met up with Colonel James Bowie's volunteers at the Mission San José y San Miguel de Aguayo. Bowie divided his men into four groups, with Salvador's unit absorbed into one of them. As they continued exploring the missions, they encountered Mexican guards and engaged them in a melee before breaking off and reforming with Bowie.[64]

Elsewhere, the spark that would ignite the Texas Revolution occurred in October 1835 over a cannon. The cannon was given to the residents of Gonzales by the Mexican army for use in securing their property against hostile Natives. When the Mexican army tried to retake possession of the artillery piece, Texians considered it an infringement on their right to arms and were determined not to relinquish the cannon.

The clash between Texan forces and the Mexican army occurred, as predicted, in Gonzalez on October 2, 1835. It was the first military engagement in the war for Texas independence. Mexican troops were driven off by the Texas volunteers and were forced back to the area around San Antonio de Béxar. The Mexican forces, led by General Martín Perfecto de Cos, numbered around 650 men. Cos fortified the plazas west of the San Antonio River and the Mission San Antonio de Valero, also known as the Alamo. The pursuing Texian forces were organized under the overall command of Stephen F. Austin. Manuel Flores was selected to be the courier to inform Austin that Seguin's volunteer company was prepared to join them at Béxar.

By the time the Texian forces had reached Salado Creek, just east of San Antonio, they had numbered four hundred men, including the company of Juan N. Seguin's Tejano volunteers.[65] It was mid-October, and while the Texians were advancing on San Antonio, General Cos had one hundred reinforcement troops brought in to help fortify his position. A debate over strategy ensued, with Sam Houston favoring caution, allowing time for further training and for cannons to be brought in to bombard Béxar fortifications. Most favored Stephen F. Austin's opinion that they should continue with a sustained siege without delay.

On October 27, from the San Fransisco de la Espada Mission, Austin dispatched Colonel James Bowie and James W. Fannin Jr. to the Nuestra Señora de la Purísima Concepción de Acuña Mission to establish a forward position. They took ninety men with them, including Salvador Flores's unit. The following day, General Cos sent 275 men under the command of Colonel Domingo de Ugarteche to attack this forward position in what was to be known as the Battle of Concepción. From an area along the bank of the San Antonio River, the Texians were able to repel the attack and capture a cannon. The Texians gained confidence, and Austin wanted to press the advantage and launch an attack on San Antonio itself, but his officer corps urged against it.

By now, reinforcements from East Texas, led by Thomas J. Rusk, had arrived, and the Texian forces had grown to an army of six hundred. There was still little support for an outright attack, and some volunteers instead opted to return home to resupply and obtain winter clothing. However, more East Texans arrived in early November to make up for the soldiers who had left.

Texian and Mexican cavalry forces engaged one another occasionally as the Texians attempted to capture supplies and gain intelligence on the Mexican movements. William B. Travis even captured three hundred Mexican mules and horses grazing past the Medina River. Despite these occasional successes, the dropping temperature and dwindling supplies were beginning to take a toll on the morale of the troops on both sides.

On November 7, 1835, the Texian Consultation issued a declaration of causes for the war against Mexico.[66,67] Soon after, three companies of over one hundred fresh troops arrived from the United States, giving Austin cause to once again push for an attack. However, with little officer support, he yielded. Stephen F. Austin chose to step down as head of the volunteer army and take up diplomatic duties in the United States. One of Austin's final commands was sent to Salvador Flores in a letter:

> Don Salvador Flores:
>
> March with your detachment to seek the detachment of Captain Fannin, which ought to be on [the] Atascosa or [the] Medina. At the ranch of Salinas or some other ranch, you ought to have news of Fannin.
>
> The object of this expedition is to discover whether it is certain that reinforcements or convoy[s] are coming to the enemy. You will also burn off the whole country from the other side of the Nueces to the Medina on the roads from Laredo and [the] Rio Grande.
>
> In case of taking public horses from the enemy, you can keep two of the best for each man of your detachment as his private property, besides those which are needed for the service. Captain Fannin will give you ten men to be joined with your detachment.
>
> Stephen F. Austin
> Conception neighborhood,
> November 14, 1835[68]

Flores's unit completed their mission and explored the Rio Grande area, reporting back on Mexican troop movement towards Béxar. Sam Houston, who was now placed in command of the army, received the report, and Edward Burleson was selected as the new leader of the Texian forces in San Antonio.

On November 26, Erastus "Deaf" Smith reported an approaching Mexican cavalry, believed to be carrying pay for the Mexican soldiers. Burleson immediately ordered units to intercept them. The Texians engaged the approaching Mexican cavalry near Alazán Creek, west of San Antonio. The Mexican troops managed to escape into the fortified area. The skirmish became known as the Grass Fight because Texian forces captured horse fodder instead of the rumored money that the captured Mexican horses were believed to have been carrying.

Supplies and morale continued to diminish, and Burleson was considering withdrawing to Goliad. However, then, a lone Mexican officer made his way out of San Antonio and surrendered to the Texian army. He spoke of low morale within the ranks of the Mexican troops as well. With this surprising news, Ben Milam and William G. Cooke rounded up over three hundred volunteers and made plans to attack the town. In the meantime, Burleson would take the remaining four hundred men and force General Cos to keep his forces divided between the Alamo and San Antonio.

Just before dawn on December 5, Captain James Clinton Neill laid down a barrage of artillery fire on the Alamo, allowing Milam and Francis W. Johnson to lead two divisions to attack the town, seizing buildings north of the plaza. Mexican cannon fire prevented the Texian forces from further advancement that day. However, that night and into the next day, Texians knocked down some buildings to give them a clearer sight of their enemy and dug trenches to connect the houses they controlled. During this period, Salvador Flores and his men engaged in house-to-house fighting. On December 7, they captured an additional house, but a sharpshooter's bullet felled Ben Milam. Johnson continued the attack the following night and captured the Navarro house. By that time, Col. Ugartechea returned with over 600 fresh reinforcement troops, though only 170 had any real experience. The others were untrained and ill-supplied. Burleson sent 100 of his men into San Antonio to join the soldiers there and helped to capture the Zambrano Row buildings. Then Cooke, with two companies, took control of the priest's home on the main plaza, though they were cut off from the rest of the Texian forces.

General Cos decided to fortify his base at the Alamo and concentrate his forces there. However, four companies of cavalry chose instead to retreat and left the area of San Antonio entirely. Morally crushed and with a disheartened army, General Cos saw the futility of continuing the battle with the reinvigorated Texians. On the morning of December 8, General Cos requested surrender terms. Burleson accepted Cos's surrender and took possession of most of the Mexican equipment and weapons. He allowed Cos and his men to withdraw to the South, mainly because the Texians were in no condition to maintain such a large group of prisoners.

Texian casualties were in the low thirties, with some estimates between thirty and thirty-five, while the Mexican forces lost about 150 men, primarily in the Morelos Infantry Battalion, charged with defending the town of San Antonio. Most historians agree this disparity in casualties is a result of greater accuracy with the Texians' rifles, which were rifled and longer than the Mexican rifles. This allowed for improved accuracy at longer ranges.[69]

After the siege had ended, and General Cos's men had left the area, most of the Texan volunteers disbanded, including Manuel Flores, and returned home. Salvador's company was dispatched to protect the ranchers from the withdrawing Mexican troops as well as any hostile Natives looking to take advantage of the situation.

San Antonio de Béxar was left under Texian control. Many feared the Mexican centralists would attempt to mount an offensive in the spring to reclaim the area. Two main roads led into the area directly from the Mexican interior. The first was the Atascosita Road, which made its way from Matamoros on the Rio Grande northward through San Patricio, Goliad, Victoria, and into the Austin colony. The other road was the Old San Antonio Road that crossed the Rio Grande at Paso de Francia and continued to the northeast directly through San Antonio de Béxar and then on to Bastrop, Nacogdoches, and across the Sabine River into Louisiana. Only two forts were defending the area along these roads: Presidio La Bahía at Goliad and the Alamo at San Antonio.

On December 21, at the behest of Sam Houston, James Clinton Neill, now commissioned a lieutenant colonel of artillery in the regular Texian army, took command of the forces at the Alamo. Lieutenant Salvador Flores and his men joined Neill at the mission, where Neill's official Alamo roster indicated Salvador was positioned as a captain of artillery. It is believed his official rank was still first lieutenant, and this might have either been a temporary brevet promotion or more of a title of command. Regardless, Salvador was now in charge of defensive artillery for the mission.

Ninety miles to the southeast, Colonel James W. Fannin Jr. took command of the troops near Goliad. With many of the veteran troops who fought at Gonzalez, Concepción, and Béxar having returned home, newly arrived American volunteers constituted a majority of the troops now serving at Goliad and Béxar. Colonels Neill and Fannin both understood that their new forces, many poorly trained and undisciplined, would not last long without experienced reinforcements in the event of a Mexican siege.

Neill made a formal request of Sam Houston for additional manpower and supplies; however, the Texian provisional government was in such turmoil that no less than four officers claimed to have been given overall command of the Texian army. By mid-January 1836, Houston sent Jim Bowie, who had since resigned his colonel's commission, to go to the Alamo and evaluate the situation. Bowie brought with him thirty men. He assured Neill that he was committed to the defense of the area. On January 22, intelligence was received that General Santa Anna was at Saltillo with approximately 3,000 Mexican troops and an advance force of 1,600 troops under the command of General Joaquin Ramirez y Sesma at Rio Grande City, progressing forward.[70] Bowie sent word to Sam Houston informing him of the advancing Mexican army, requesting additional troops and supplies to defend the Alamo.

A veteran of Gonzalez, newly commissioned Lieutenant Colonel William B. Travis arrived at the Alamo on February 3, 1836, with twenty-five men. However, soon after, Neill received word that his mother had grown deathly ill, and he was needed to return home to see to her care. After some tension between Travis and Bowie, who

believed as a former colonel he should not answer to Travis, a lieutenant colonel, Neill officially left the garrison under the joint command of Lieutenant Colonel William B. Travis and Jim Bowie, effective February 12. A few days prior, on February 8, former Tennessee
congressman and famed frontiersman David Crocket arrived with
sixteen additional volunteers. On February 10, a party was held in
honor of Crockett. It was during this party that a courier came with
news that the Mexican armies of Santa Anna and Sesma had linked
up and were ready to march on Béxar. Travis believed it would take
approximately thirteen days for the army to arrive.

On February 23, 1836, the threat was confirmed when Mexican
forces under the command of General Antonio López de Santa Anna
began their siege upon the Texian garrison at the Alamo. Around the
time of the initial siege, Seguin arrived with some additional troops,
including Manuel Flores. Shortly after his arrival, Seguin was selected
to get a message through enemy lines back to the other Texian forces
informing them that the Alamo defenders would neither retreat nor surrender. Sometime after Seguin's departure, General Santa Anna called a
three-day armistice. It is believed that during that time, the Flores brothers, Salvador and Manuel, left the Alamo to check on their families, who
had been left alone. After ensuring the safety of their families, the brothers regrouped and recruited additional volunteers from the area.

Two of those volunteers were Jose Maria Flores and Nepomuceno
Flores, brothers of Manuel and Salvador. Nepomuceno, youngest
of the four, was born Jose Maria Victoriano Nepomuceno Flores
on September 5, 1811, in La Villa de San Fernando de Béxar. He
enlisted and served as a corporal under Seguin in the Texian volunteer army. Jose Maria, actually a few years older than Salvador, was
born Jose Maria Victoriano Flores de Abrego in 1804 in La Villa de
San Fernando de Béxar. He served as a private in his brother Manuel's
Company B until June 10, 1836.

By early March 1836, these new volunteers met up with Seguin
in Gonzales. The company was reorganized with Seguin appoint-
ing Manuel Flores as his company first sergeant. The group then
proceeded west to reinforce the Alamo defenders. They made their
way to Cibolo, where they were to link up with Colonel Fannin's

troops. Fannin never arrived, and the Alamo fell on March 6, with all defenders having been killed after a bloody thirteen-day siege, long before Seguin and the Flores brothers were ever able to return.

Unfortunately, unbeknownst to Seguin, Colonel Fannin was up against intense enemy pressure. On March 19, Fannin and his Texian garrison retreated from Presidio La Bahia but surrendered after fierce fighting the following day at the Battle of Coleto. The captured Fannin, and his Texian troops were taken back to Goliad where they were all executed on March 27, 1836, under orders of General Santa Anna.

As Captain Seguin's troops left Gonzales, Lieutenant Salvador Flores would assume command of the western rear guard, protecting fleeing ranchers and their families as the Texian forces proceeded to secure the lower ranches of San Antonio.[71]

Seguin's forces would now split up. Salvador would maintain his position protecting from any rear attack. Seguin, with First Sergeant Manuel Flores, alongside his brothers, Corporal Nepomuceno Flores and Private Jose Flores, continued onward to follow in General Sam Houston's advance eastward. Seguin and Salvador successfully blocked the Mexican army from crossing the Brazos River, preventing them from overtaking the Texian forces. They would link up with General Sam Houston's army along with General Thomas Jefferson Rusk's army at the Battle of San Jacinto and the successful defeat of Santa Anna's Mexican army.

It is Sergeant Manuel Flores who is credited for leading the final charge against the Mexican forces at San Jacinto. In his book *Rodriguez Memoirs of Early Texas*, José Maria Rodriguez states that during the final charge, the Texians fired an artillery volley and then hit the ground in anticipation of return fire from the Mexicans. Only Manuel Flores remained standing and issued a challenge to the other troops, "Get up, you cowards. Santa Ana's men are running." The Texians, following Flores, pursued the withdrawing Mexicans. A cease-fire was called, and the men rounded up approximately six hundred Mexican troops as prisoners. Within a few days, General Santa Anna himself was taken prisoner, and the main Mexican Army was finished.[72]

In May 1836, Juan Seguin was promoted to lieutenant colonel. As a representative of an independent Texas, he then accepted the Mexican surrender of San Antonio and the Alamo on June 4, 1836. He remained there as military commander until the fall of 1837, directing the burial services of the gallant Alamo defenders.

The official muster rolls of December 1836 indicate Salvador Flores was now a captain in San Antonio commanding Company C, Second Cavalry Regiment, in the Regular Army of Texas, under the command of Lieutenant Colonel Juan Seguin. In a letter addressed to Seguin dated November 24, 1835, written by Stephen F. Austin, it was Captain Flores who was singled out as a "patriot" in the fight for Texas independence. In the years after the Texas Revolution, Salvador remained a force for justice and protector of the ranchers and settlers of Texas.

According to his service record no. 4220, the official muster rolls of December 1836 also indicate Manuel Flores was now a first lieutenant in San Antonio commanding Company B, Second Cavalry Regiment, and later as captain from March 1 to October 12, 1837, in the Regular Army of Texas under the command of Lieutenant Colonel Juan Seguin.[73]

In 1838, after his military service concluded, Manuel Flores started a ranch on the south side of the Guadalupe River, across from the city of Seguin, having been established out of Guadalupe County just a little over a year after the Texas Revolution. The ranch was near a natural rock waterfall that came to be known as the Flores Falls. The Flores ranch became one of the larger working ranches of the period.

Having returned to power after his loss in the Texas Revolution, Santa Anna wasn't finished with Texas just yet. On March 5, 1842, Santa Anna sent General Rafael Vásquez and a Mexican army of seven hundred men to march on San Antonio. The city was ill prepared to repel the invasion and fell almost without a fight. General Vásquez raised the Mexican flag and declared San Antonio once again under the laws of Mexico. Having been elected mayor of San Antonio just the year prior, Juan Seguin was mired in baseless claims that he was pro-Mexico and had secretly lent aid to them.[74] Seguin and many citizens of San Antonio fled the city and found refuge on the ranch of Manuel Flores in Seguin, Texas.[75] There, Salvador Flores joined the pair, and a counterattack was planned. They formed a volunteer unit to pursue General Vásquez's army as they began their withdrawal from San Antonio on March 7.[76]

Though Mexican forces returned across the border and the whole incursion was considered by the Republic of Texas as a guerilla raid, Seguin was forced to resign as mayor of San Antonio that April. The false charges that he was pro-Mexico were too much to bear. Due to death threats, Seguin fled to Mexico, where he was promptly arrested and pressed into military service as an officer in the Mexican army. In what was sure to be a great indignation for Seguin, he was assigned as a staff officer in the expeditionary army of General Adrián Woll tasked with once again marching on San Antonio.[77]

President Santa Anna directed Vásquez's incursion, and now he had ordered General Woll to capture San Antonio again and probe down the Guadalupe River to Gonzales. There was no political gain, and the only purpose appeared to be to harass the Texans and gain face with Mexican officials.

Woll entered San Antonio on September 11. The Flores ranch was once again being used as a refuge for fleeing San Antonio citizens. By September 18, Woll was defeated by the Texas army in the Battle of Salado Creek, and his forces completely withdrew from San Antonio within two days. The Mexican invasion was considered as a plundering by a criminal renegade, but it did lead to the Somervell and Mier military expeditions, which Texas president Sam Houston had ordered to pursue the retreating Mexican army and then invade Mexico if the situation seemed favorable. Ultimately, the expeditions failed, and the Texas troops returned home.

The Flores brothers returned home as well. Around 1840, Nepomuceno married Margarita Josefa Valdes, daughter of Serapio Valdes and Josefa Farias. Official Bexar County records indicate Nepomuceno Flores received a headright certificate under the authority of the Republic of Texas for one league and one labor of land, roughly 4,605.5 acres, issued on May 11, 1838. Muster rolls show Nepomuceno as a corporal in Seguin's volunteer Texian Company that fought at the battle of San Jacinto. For participating in that battle, he received Donation Certificate No. 182 granting him 640 acres of land as well as Bounty Certificate No. 3487 for 1,280 acres of land due him for military service. Service Record No. 4223 certifies that he was commissioned a first lieutenant on October 14, 1836, in the army of the Republic of Texas, serving until his discharge on May 15, 1838. Nepomuceno joined the Texas Veterans Association and died in Wilson County around December 2, 1878, although some sources say he lived until sometime in 1881.

Salvador Flores returned to private life and married Maria Clara Flores on May 24, 1841. Maria Clara passed some time before 1848; hence, Salvador married Concepcion Rojo on September 30, 1848, in San Antonio. They had two children in addition to the five he had with Maria Clara. He spent the remainder of his life around San Antonio and died there on January 17, 1855. Juan Seguin was appointed guardian of his family and administrator of his estate.

In 1853, Manuel Flores sold his ranch and began a new one in Atascosa County. Unfortunately, his wife, Maria, died the following year. Around 1858, he married Margarita Garza. He became a mason in Alamo Lodge 44. He lived peacefully until his death on December 3, 1868.

Though the memoirs of Juan Seguin indicate that all four of the Flores brothers fought alongside him during the Texas Revolution, Jose Maria does not show up on any muster rolls for any of the Texas battles. No records found indicate he was ever granted any headright or bounty certificates for his military services. He was also the only Flores brother not promoted to officer in the newly commissioned Republic of Texas army. Some historians believe that when the other elder brothers were fighting, Jose's duty was to stay behind to look after the family and maintain the family ranch. It wasn't until early 1836 that Jose joined the Texian volunteer army, joining his brothers at Gonzales and then fighting alongside them until June 10, 1836, upon which time he returned home to the family ranch. He married Maria Lionides Seguin in June 1831. The couple had five children. It is believed Jose Maria Flores died in San Antonio on December 3, 1868.[78]

The legacy of the Flores brothers is far-reaching. It was Salvador's skill as a *vaquero* and horseback cavalry tactics that would be proven effective in skirmish after skirmish throughout the Texas Revolution, so much so that his tactics were rumored to be modeled by the Texas Rangers. In 1867, Josefa Agustina Flores de Abrego, daughter of Jose Maria and wife of Wilson County's first sheriff, Samuel William Barker, donated two hundred acres of family land to Wilson County. The county commissioner's court accepted the donation and was selected as the new county seat. Per her request, the new area was dubbed Floresville in honor of her great-great-grandfather, Francisco Antonio Flores de Abrego II. A Texas State historical marker was placed at the Floresville courthouse in 1986 in honor of the Flores family for their distinguished service to Texas.[79]

Juan Seguin, having returned to Mexico and been pressed into military service, continued to serve under Santa Anna in the Mexican-American War of 1846. In February 1848, he requested formal permission to return home to Texas. His request was granted, and by 1852, Seguin had settled near his father's house in Floresville. He was elected and served two terms as Bexar County justice of the peace. In 1869, he served as county judge of Wilson County. By 1883, Seguin had been conducting business on occasion in Nuevo Laredo, Tamaulipas, Mexico. As his son Santiago was mayor, Seguin decided to relocate there permanently. He died in Nuevo Laredo on August 27, 1890. His body was returned to Texas in 1974 as part of the American bicentennial celebration, and he was reinterred in the city of Seguin during the July 4 ceremony. A statue of Seguin, astride with saber drawn, now stands in the Seguin Central Park downtown in honor of his service.

On March 7, 2018, the Juan N. Seguin Historic Park was dedicated in La Porte, Texas, near the San Jacinto Battleground State Historic Site. The park, spanning five acres along the Houston Ship Channel, honors the brave men who fought under Seguin's command at San Jacinto, with each volunteer's name recognized and honored on one of the markers spread out across the park.

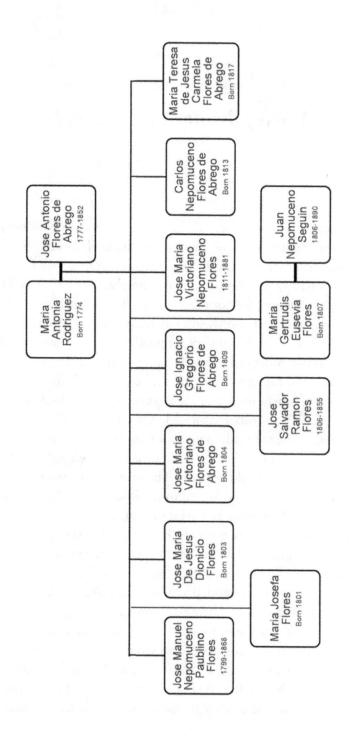

A Brief History of Rockport

"The Charm of the Texas Coast," the beautiful beach city of Rockport is settled along the Gulf of Mexico on State Highway 35.[80] The county seat of Aransas County, the city resides on Live Oak Peninsula between Copano and Aransas Bays, just northeast of Corpus Christi.

The city was named for the rocky shelf at the core of its shoreline and was founded shortly after the Civil War. Now known for tourism and its fishing industry, originally, the area was primarily used as a cattle processing and shipping port. Cattleman William S. Hall built the first processing plants here in 1865 and, in its first eight years of operation, processed some four hundred thousand heads of cattle.[81] In 1866, James M. Doughty and Richard Wood constructed immense cattle pens as a staging area for slaughtering. In 1867, John M. and Thomas H. Mathis joined Doughty in forming their own cattle packing plant. The group was then joined that same year by Col. George W. Fulton, son-in-law of former governor Henry Smith. Fulton had relocated his family from Maryland back to the Rockport area, where he had previously served as customs director for the General Land Office. Together, the group formed the Coleman, Mathis, Fulton Cattle Company in 1871.[82]

Rockport was incorporated as a town in 1870 and later as a city in 1871, with John Mathis being appointed by the governor as the city's first mayor. This was the same year that Aransas County lines were drawn out of the larger Refugio County. Mathis and his partners' cattle company owned 115,000 acres and played an active role in the economic boom that was beginning to roll out in Rockport. In 1879, Mathis sold his interest in the company, which was renamed the Coleman-Fulton Pasture Company (Fulton). By the end of the 1870s, Rockport was home to a dozen beef slaughterhouses, known as packeries.[83]

However, markets change. It was once the single largest cattle processor in Texas, but the expansion of the railroad was making it easier for cattle to be transported around the country. The number of cattle needed to be sent through Rockport began to lessen. Business declined. This was a significant concern, and David Sinton, having gained majority control of Coleman-Fulton, ended up having to sell its wharf, cattle pens, and warehouses. George Fulton died in 1893, but the company continued in some fashion and remained an economic staple of the area until 1930.

A state historical marker was erected as a reminder of the impact the cattle industry had on Rockport in its early days. The only other remnant of that past is the mansion built in 1877 by packery co-owner George Fulton, which resides in the town so named for him. Though many hurricanes have blown through, the Fulton Mansion stands tall as an architecturally unique home and historic site. It remains under the care of the Texas Historical Commission.[84]

In the 1880s, with the decline of the cattle processing industry, boatbuilding and fishing soon grew into important local industries. As a result, the tourism trade flourished, and residents began to invest in the possibility of a deepwater harbor. This would require a channel to be created through the sandbar at Aransas Pass. However, due to soured investments, the community had to endure an economic slump. Interest in the deepwater port continued, and numerous projects were undertaken, specifically in 1884, 1905, and 1910. In 1921, Robert J. Kleberg Sr., head of the King Ranch, called a meeting in Kingsville regarding a new project to finish the harbor. From that meeting, an appointee named Roy Miller was dispatched to Washington, DC, to lobby for assistance in completing the deepwater port. The following year, President Warren G. Harding signed a bill creating a new port in Corpus Christi, not Rockport.[85]

The Aransas County Courthouse, designed by prominent Texas architect J. Riely Gordon, was completed in 1889. Electric lights were installed throughout the city the following year. The beautiful courthouse was used continuously until a new courthouse was erected in 1956.

Rockport is also known for the nearby wildlife sanctuary and is located along the Texas Tropical Trail as well as the Great Texas Coastal Birding Trail. In 1907, Governor Thomas M. Campbell appointed R. H. Wood as the state's first game, fish, and oyster Commissioner, responsible for revising the wildlife laws. Wood was empowered to draft new conservation laws governing fish and to now include game, namely, small winged and ground animals but also larger animals, such as deer and antelope.[86]

The Aransas National Wildlife Refuge, just northeast of Rockport, created in 1937, was the first federal refuge established in Texas. This beautiful area of tidal marshes provides a secure area for waterfowl to find sanctuary, chiefly the whooping crane, which can be found there during the winter months. The whooping crane, a symbol for conservation, represents the area's sustained efforts to protect endangered wildlife through habitat preservation, hunting restrictions, breeding, and releasing programs.[87] Then in 1967, the Connie Hagar Wildlife Sanctuary was established within the city limits of Rockport. For about five weeks a year, it is a prime location to watch several different species of hummingbird feed on local flower nectar and insects.[88]

The Rockport Chamber of Commerce was organized in 1912, but its efforts to develop the town were halted in 1919 by a hurricane that nearly leveled the community. Recovery was slow. In 1935, the Aransas County Navigation District built harbors at Rockport and Fulton as well as the Rockport Beach and the saltwater swimming pool, a protected area off Aransas Bay. That same year, the city finally got their port.[89]

With the demise of the local cattle economy, the shrimping industry developed between 1925 and 1930 and became a significant boon for the city in the 1940s. Later that decade, the industry slowed, but in the 1950s, it was successful again. The boatbuilding trade also picked up during this time. T. Noah Smith Sr. founded the Rockport Yacht and Supply Company in 1935. A vertical-lift turntable and trackage were installed in 1950. Around 1967, one of these new turntables claimed the life of one of my uncles, Francisco Molina, who was working at Rockport Yacht & Supply.

In the 1960s, the company began a thriving trade in steel-hulled boats. Rob Roy Rice started another shipyard in 1941 to build submarine chasers for the war effort. However, after the war, business slowed, and Rice's yard eventually shut down.

The population of Rockport grew steadily over the years. In 1914, the town had a reported population of 1,382. By the early 1940s, the number of residents had increased to 1,729, and the city had sixty-five businesses. In 1970, the reported population had doubled to 3,900, and the companies numbered 150. This can be partially attributed to the influx of Vietnamese refugees fleeing the conflict in Southeast Asia. Many found work as "day shrimpers."

By 1980, the population was 3,686, and in 1986, it was estimated at 5,120. The major sources of commerce in Rockport remained the fishing and shrimping industries, along with the tourist trade. Vacationers could relax and fish, swim, watch birds, visit the wildlife refuges, and enjoy other attractions like Goose Island and the Fulton Mansion. The annual Rockport Art Festival in July and Seafair in October are huge attractions. The Rockport Art Center, which provides gallery space for the many local artists, is also a great place to visit. Rockport has several historic homes from the cattle-market days, and the Sisters of Schoenstatt Convent (1959) and the Chapel of Our Lady, Star of the Sea (1958), the oldest church in the area, are located only minutes away in nearby Lamar. The restaurant and motel trades also provide much of the city's commercial life. In 1990, the population dropped slightly to 4,753, but grew to 7,385 by 2000. In the years following, the population grew to around 10,000.

In the overnight hours of August 26, 2017, Hurricane Harvey, a category 4 storm, slammed into Rockport, causing devastation and anguish to the many residents that call the coastal area home. High winds, heavy rains, and flooding inundated the area, knocking down trees, signs, homes, buildings, and businesses. The devastation was widespread, with a hotel wall collapsing, windows being blown out of police cars, and vintage buildings being erased from existence.

More than half of the residents chose to stay in their homes in an attempt to weather the storm. Approximately a dozen were injured, and at least one person perished in a home fire. First responders tried their best to rescue those in dire need, but they found themselves under siege by the deluge of heavy rain and winds. Some of those rescued reported their roofs being ripped off their homes, walls falling in on themselves, and the sound of a freight train bearing down on them. Despite the pain and devastation, Rockport is a resilient city, determined to rebuild and reclaim their coastal charm.[90]

Months after the storm, late January 2018, I visited Rockport. There were still no open hotels and only one restaurant open, though most of that was still under construction. As I drove around, I ventured down Highway 35 where I witnessed, in the median between the eastbound and westbound lanes, at least a mile-long collection of debris piled dozens of feet high. Every couple hundred feet or so sat huge incinerators with glowing red plumes as the debris that was once someone's belongings was being reduced to ashes. It was hard to imagine that mile-long pile was once someone's home, someone's toys, someone's memories.

My mother had just recently sold her retirement home and moved to live with my sister in San Antonio. Her quiet neighborhood sat only 1,000 feet or so from Fulton Harbor. She returned the same weekend I did and found the area shattered. The storage building where she left a few small containers of belongings to pick up later was utterly destroyed. As she walked the debris, she found the remains of some of her old pictures and books. It was quite heart-wrenching; however, at the same time, there was optimism. The family was gathering; there was an overflow of love and compassion in the air.

That night, as I sat with one of my cousins in the only restaurant open for business, Paradise Key Dockside Bar & Grill, I was looking around at the residents all making the best of what they had. While workers toiled hard in other parts of the building, making it ready for operation, we could see the staff running back and forth to a makeshift kitchen built outside. When I asked the server how she was coping with the aftermath, she paused and sighed. She said that while what happened was horrible, it could've been worse. Rather than dwell on the storm, she said her family preferred to look to the future, to the possibilities for a new Rockport.

This sentiment was true for many who chose to remain living in Rockport after the storm. It was estimated that approximately 20 percent of residents permanently relocated away from Rockport after the hurricane; however, most would remain and rebuild. Construction companies had been working full-time completing repairs and building new homes, piers, boat lifts, and businesses. When I see each photo of a newly completed fishing pier, dock, or house, I know Rockport is going to be okay. The community has been through too much to give up. The city will rebound better than ever.

Family Anecdotes and Remembrances of Rockport

Coming Home
A Nava Family History in Narrative
by Rosa Nava Krinsky

As I sipped my tall latte, my thoughts were rambling. Highway 59 from Houston seemed extraordinarily long and desolate. I was coming home. I was coming home for good. Dad had been more than what Mom could handle, and with all the local siblings working or with their own demanding families, any available help was desperately needed. I was a prime candidate for the job. I could lend Mom some assistance so she could at least go to the game room to play her eight-liners for a few hours a week. Playing the eight-liners relaxed her where she would temporarily forget her burdens at home. Plus, I was looking forward to coming home. To see those still around from my school years and those whom I was still close to and considered family as well as my own large family that still lived in town.

My thoughts were running amok, back to the early days when I first came to Rockport. It was a small family then, and I was only three years old. Dad was a fifth-generation Texan. His great-great-great-grandfather was one of the original Canary Islanders who came in 1731 and settled in San Fernando de Béxar. The family basically stayed in Bexar County and slowly migrated with the railroad to Atascosa County, San Patricio County, and finally to Aransas County. Although Dad was born in Rockport, he left town after the war to live in Alice, Texas, with his new wife, Clara, and new baby girl, Yolli, my older sister.

His in-laws were originally from Alice, but Longina and Enrique, Mom's parents, had been living in Rockport temporarily due to a contract Enrique had with Heldenfeld building a shipyard at the end of what is now Water Street. My father's mother was named Medarda, or Lola as she was called. Dad called her MaLala, and us, well, as young children, we called her MaLala, and the name stuck. Even my kids still called her by that name years later. MaLala and Longina became fast friends and often talked about their children "getting together." Dad had a neighbor friend named Stella Flores that he was wooing, and Lola was very possessive of Dad. At one point, Dad eloped with Stella, and they took off to live with Stella's family, Doña Consuelo, across from the *placeta*. When Dad didn't come home, MaLala took off with a broomstick and got him out of that house, chasing Dad with that stick all the way home. Later, it was known that Stella was carrying Dad's baby. When MaLala found out, it was all she could do to get Dad married off to anyone else other than Stella.

Luckily for her, the war was going on, and most of the men were going to be shipped off to fight. So Dad got married to Mom, Clara Molina Munoz, even though Stella was carrying his baby. Mom and Dad had spoken of the situation, and she had offered to take the baby and raise him. MaLala would have no part of it. She said she would disown him if he helped Stella in any way.

So Dad went off to war. He was inducted into the US Army on June 22, 1944, at Fort Sam Houston in San Antonio. After basic training, he was assigned to a light artillery gun crew. By early 1945, he received his orders—he was leaving for Europe. He began his journey on February 3, 1945, and arrived with some of the first units of his division at Camp Old Gold in Limésy, France, on February 12, 1945. Dad had been assigned to the Second Platoon, Cannon Company, of the Seventy-First Division Artillery, Seventy-First Infantry Division.

His unit moved east and saw their first action on March 11, 1945, working to push the Germans out of France. They advanced through Germany, from Bas-Rihn, Moselle, Pfalz, Hessen-Nassau, on through Thuringia and Bavaria before stopping in the Ober-Oesterreich region of Austria. The war was over, and with many of his unit, he was demobilized. After serving a total of five months and eighteen days in Europe, Dad was coming home. He left Austria on July 15, 1945, arriving back in the United States on July 20, 1945.[91]

For his wartime service, Dad was awarded the Combat Infantryman Badge, a Bronze Star, and a Good Conduct Medal, in addition to a handful of service medals for his participation in both the Rhineland and Central Europe campaigns. His unit was assigned to Camp Chaffee, Arkansas, to await formal separation. Private First Class Rudy Nava was officially discharged on April 25, 1946.

Once he returned home from Europe, just before reporting to Camp Chafee, Dad was granted some furlough time to visit his family in Rockport. He had saved up quite a bit of money for the arrival of his child with Stella. However, with MaLala looking over his shoulder, he was forbidden from giving any of it to her.

Instead, he purchased an empty house that MaLala had her eye on. It was next door to her sister Tomasita Nava Rinche's home. Dad paid $500 cash for it. MaLala took a bus to Corpus Christi to find house movers who could relocate the home to a new location for her. The site where it was resettled is now the warehouse of Bracht's Lumber Co.

Back when Dad was home briefly after completing army basic training, before being shipped overseas, Mom got pregnant. When Dad returned home a year later, after the war, his new daughter was eight months old.

There was too much going on in Rockport, especially with a new son, Anthony, whom he was forbidden to see. Rudy decided to move his growing family, now including his baby daughter Maria Yolanda, or Yolli, to Alice to live with Mom's parents, who had moved back. Once in Alice, Mom could get the help she needed, especially now with another baby on the way. Mom was the eldest of her sisters and helped her mother, Longina, with the younger six children. She could not just abandon her responsibilities just because she went off and got married at the age of fourteen. So the family lived with Longina or, as we called her, Buelita.

Soon, a son was born on March 1, 1947, Rodolfo Enrique, and then a year later, I, Rosa came into this world on July 15, 1948. You know, growing up, Spanish was forbidden to be spoken in school, at least where we grew up. My name was anglicized to Rose; my brother was simply Rudy Jr., but we called him the Baby Boy, or just Baby Boy.

While Mom was about due to give birth to me, her father, Enrique, took deathly ill and was taken to Hermann Hospital in Houston. There he had surgery but never regained consciousness from the anesthesia. On the day he died, I was but eight days old. Dad had to take a bus to Houston to be with his father-in-law alone since Mom had the three little ones at home.

After Grandpa Enrique died, Dad picked up stakes and took his mother, MaLala; his mother-in-law, Longina; and all the children to nearby Premont, where he found work at Storm Nursery. It was a good job. He worked planting shrubbery and trees throughout Jim Wells County. Every time we passed the Premont School, we see the giant trees Dad planted as little seedlings and always say, "Daddy planted those trees when they were small twigs."

Mom worked the small farm, while the grandmothers cared for all the children. After Nelda was born in 1950, MaLala wanted to come home to see her father, who had stayed behind. One of MaLala's sisters, Virginia, was moving to a new house with her husband, Tio Goyo. Virginia, or Tia Nina as we called her, was moving her brood of eight to Live Oak Street. Dad took the opportunity and quickly moved in with Tia Nina. It was a one-bedroom house with a kitchen in the back. The living room and the bedroom were all in one big front room. It had a covered front porch where the family sat in the evenings to watch the children play and cool off from the daily grind in the usual South Texas hot heat. That empty house still stands on Front Street in Rockport.

MaLala had gone to live down the street in a two-room house to be close to her father, Eugene, who was now ninety years old. That was the house that Dad had built in late 1943 right before he went off to fight in Europe. Since a fourth child was on board and a fifth on the way, the need for a bigger house was a fast-arising need. He knew he could not stay in Tia Nina's house for long.

With only an eighth-grade education, Dad got a job at Picton's Lumber Yard unloading cargo trains and was quickly promoted to inside sales. Before he knew it, he was managing the entire store, ordering merchandise and responsible for all the outside laborers. I remember many a Sunday when the phone would ring, hearing someone on the other end pleading, "I'm only here for a day, and I have some home repairs I need to do right now. Can you please open the lumberyard for me?" Dad was never one to say no, so off he went, right in the middle of Sunday dinner to sell a few dollars' worth of lumber to some rich tourist from who knows where. That was commonplace for Saturday and Sunday afternoons. One Saturday a month, it was a relief when we had to go into Corpus Christi to get away from the phone.

Picton's Lumber Yard closed at noon on Saturday, so by that time, Mom would have us all bathed and dressed, ready to hightail it to Corpus Christi to get our monthly fare before the phone started to ring for Dad to go back to the yard. Our monthly trip to the HEB in Corpus was a big event even though we stayed in the car while Mom and Dad went inside. Unbeknownst to them, we looked like a bunch of monkeys hanging out the car window. We would climb out of the car through the windows even as we recalled being threatened that our feet better not touch that pavement or else! We would sit or stand on the window, climb on the car roof, or climb over the car via the windows—generally be a nuisance. However, our feet never touched the ground as we were warned not to do.

Mom and Dad would get their usual bushel of cucumbers, tomatoes, grapefruit, and oranges, cases of canned vegetables, a big sack of onions, a five-gallon tin of lard, a twenty-pound sack of flour, and a twenty-pound bag of rice. Sometimes, there was even a roast or two and plenty of calf livers. The fabric in which the flour came in was very important. Buelita's next quilt or our next summer dress could be made out of it. The perishables we would get weekly at the local Roe's Food Store in Rockport. With Rockport's primary industry being fishing and shrimping, seafood was usually on the daily menu. Since it was free for the asking, we survived on oysters, shrimp, red snapper, flounder, and crabs—not a bad way to dine, thinking back.

Sometimes, we would kill a chicken from the chicken coop in the backyard. That was where we got our eggs daily. I remember, as a child, during oyster season, Dad would have a dump truck drop a truckload of oysters on our dirt driveway, just inside our white fence. Dad's drinking buddies and compadres would sit around the mound on a little makeshift stool or brick with their Falstaff beer by their side shucking oysters for their families. They would drop them in gallon pickle jars and every now and again would let one slide down their throat with a swig of beer. Now being that they were in our front yard, we were usually playing around the oyster mound or just "walking the fence" as we called it. It gave us a reason to harass Dad into letting us have an oyster also. By the time Dad had one and gave each of us one, it was time for him to have another and start all over again with us. I guess it was no wonder why he always ended up with a jug or two of oysters, while the other men always had several. We would not eat dinner that night and usually had a bellyache by the evening.

You know for the entire time we lived in Rockport back then, we had the same telephone number, Southfield 4-6206. I think all of Rockport knew that number, but Dad refused to disconnect the phone or change the number for fear that someone might need his help and not be able to locate him. That was Dad. I don't know why he worried. Rockport was a small town with a population of less than one thousand back then, and everyone and their dog knew where we lived. Once our neighbor Jesus's car caught fire, and they reported it to the volunteer fire department. The standard procedure was to post the location on a blackboard mounted on the front of the firehouse. Since they did not know who our neighbor was on the posting for the ensuing fire, they wrote "Rudy's house." They knew that the firemen would drive to Rudy's house and see the neighbor's car ablaze. We got calls for days asking us about our burned house, and we had to explain it was the neighbor's car.

Dad was well-known and well-liked as he was involved in several local organizations. He was president of the first Hispanic Lions Club ever established. In the mid-50s, shrimping was a big business, if not the only business, where someone with limited to no education could make a decent living. Most of the shrimpers or fishermen were members; hence, they were called the Seamen's Lions Club. All the events they sponsored were to help the needy Hispanic families in the area. They collected eyeglasses for those that couldn't afford them. They sponsored events to give small token scholarships to the few Hispanics who were fortunate to graduate and helped on election days to drive those with no transportation to the polls.

Not only did Dad work at Picton's Lumber Yard all day, from 8:00 a.m. to 5:00 p.m., he would also get up at five in the morning to go turn the sprinklers on at the Donnellys' home, who lived in Fulton. The Donnellys lived in San Antonio but came to Rockport on the weekends, so Dad kept their yard maintained during their absence. He would pull the few stray weeds, dodge the dollar weeds, feed the birds, and throw out a few nuts for the squirrels. He had to be sure to be home by 7:30 a.m. to eat a quick breakfast that Mom had already cooked for all the kids, including her siblings since her father's death. Since Mom was the oldest, her younger siblings looked up to Dad as their father. They also saw Mom as their mother as she was the main person in their lives. Buelita was a seamstress at Fashion Cleaners in Alice and was hardly home due to a long work schedule.

By this time, Dad was well established at the lumberyard, so he was able to get materials at cost directly from the vendors and pay for them on a payment plan. Many of the local Hispanics owed Dad many, many favors because Daddy always looked out for the under-dog. He made sure they had jobs, change in their pockets, and food on their table. Meanwhile, Dad himself had to take several side jobs gardening to make ends meet for his own family. With his growing family, he could feel the need for a bigger house was quickly coming their way.

By early 1951, a new two-bedroom house was built with the help of all his buddies who owed him. We moved in our few belongings. Dad went to Corpus Christi with Mom and purchased a wooden dinette set with four chairs, a couch covered in brown vinyl with a big head of a longhorn embroidered on the back, along with a matching club chair. He took out a line of credit at Braslaw's, which took him years to pay off at five dollars a month. We now had an actual living room and inside plumbing!

Just as we got a little extra room, Mom got pregnant again. She asked her sister, Gloria, who was graduating high school in Alice, to come live with us. She could help Mom out, and it would be good for her to spread her wings. Aunt Gloria agreed and moved in. She would sleep in the front bedroom with Yolli and me. The Baby Boy was five years old now. He would sleep on the couch. The back had hinges that unlocked so the back could be laid flat to become a bed. Since it was vinyl, the sheets would slip off as we tossed and turned, making it hotter during the night. The youngest at the time was Nelda, and she slept between Mom and Dad. That wouldn't last long, for in a few months, another sibling would join the troops, and Nelda would be shifted to sleep with Aunt Gloria in the other room. The new baby would now sleep in the middle of Mom and Dad. Norma Anna was born in June of 1951. The Baby Boy still had the couch to himself. Lucky him.

On January 4, 1951, Great-Grandpa Eugene was killed crossing the street to visit his eldest daughter, Tomasita, or Chita as he called her. His skull was fractured when he was struck by a truck. Since MaLala was now alone, she asked if Yolli could stay with her for company. That would help Mom out since she now had five children at home. Hesitatingly, she half agreed, not because she didn't want Yolli to go, but that would mean Dad would have to go over there more often, which meant time away from home. It was a great help though. MaLala spoiled Yolli rotten and waited on her hand and foot. She did have her house rules, but for the most part, Yolli got everything she needed and wanted. When it was freezing outside, she would warm her socks up on the gas heater along the wall and put her socks on her while she was still under the covers and often still asleep. She would even dress her and wash her face while still sleeping because she didn't want to rouse her from her slumber. She would hand-starch and iron her dresses and petticoats so stiff they looked like lifelike mannequins standing in the corner. She would wear little hats to church on Sundays with matching clutch bags. We would pick her up on Sunday morning to go to church, and I felt jealous with Yolli with her black patent leather shoes. I don't know why I was so envious; I was next in line from the girls to get her hand-me-downs. I could be assured she would wear them gently because MaLala was a stickler about that. My clothes would be passed on to Nelda, and

Nelda's would be passed on to the new addition, Norma. Lucky Baby Boy was the only boy. He got new clothes or at least hand-me-downs from an outsider, which could be considered new to us.

Well, soon, Baby Boy was no longer the only boy in the family. In 1952, my little brother Hector Eugene was born. He was named after Great-Grandpa Eugene who had passed the previous year. Sleeping arrangements changed again; Norma would now sleep with Aunt Gloria, Nelda, and me. Hector would take center stage between Mom and Dad. The Baby Boy had the couch to himself pretty much all the time unless we had company, like Buelita and her new husband, Manuel Soza, from Alice. In that case, all the girls would sleep on the opened couch with Aunt Gloria and Aunt Gloria's youngest sister, Aunt Alma. The Baby Boy would then have to endure the cold linoleum floor with only a blanket spread beneath him. Luckily for him, that didn't happen very often.

Mom and Dad both had green thumbs, so they worked on the yard and took great pride in their work. We had a wire fence around our house with flower beds all along the edges that were always in bloom. I don't remember a day that we did not have fresh flowers inside the house. Two palm trees along with a mulberry tree were gifted to us from the neighbor across the street, Mr. Emory Spencer. He had sent his gardener over to plant them for us. He was a nice man.

With Aunt Gloria at home to care for us and Mom having her tubes tied after Hector was born, the family-making machine was pretty much out of commission. She could now, or rather had to now, help Dad in whatever way she could to put food on the table.

Mom began to clean houses for the wealthier residents who bought homes in Rockport but only used them on weekends or holidays. We called them winter Texans. She had a few clients—the Donnellys, the Kleins, and the Kaltairs. While Dad maintained their yards, Mom kept the insides dust free. On Saturdays, she would take the whole brood with her to the Klein's. While Dad worked in the yard, we climbed trees, ran around the yard, and became Dad's go'fers (go for this, go for that). We would help feed the squirrels and fill the bird feeders. Occasionally, we had to help pull weeds or move the sprinklers to a new location. As long as we stayed out of the house and out of Mom's way, we pretty much had the run of the outside.

The Kleins had a flat roof, and it was fenced. They had a staircase leading up to it. There were pebbles on the roof. Beats me why anyone would want to go up there and walk on a hot pebbled roof, except us of course. A fig tree hugged the rooftop, so we could easily reach the top figs before the birds got to them.

By 1954, Mom had three of us starting school. The Kleins were the most generous. The first year I went to school, they took Yolli, the Baby Boy, and me shopping for a new set of school clothes at Lichtenstein's, the fanciest store in Corpus Christi. We got to try on clothes and more or less pick whatever we wanted. That first year, I chose a pair of pink suede loafers, a dark-blue pleated wool skirt with suspenders, and a pink button-down blouse with a Peter Pan collar and puffed sleeves. It had a design embroidered on the left upper corner with a see-through netting the size of a quarter. I was so stylish; I had a see-through blouse that I bragged about. My loafers were a size too big; Mom said that was so I could grow into them and therefore last the entire school year. I loved those shoes, although I almost didn't have them long.

I was so proud of those shoes that something was destined to happen to them. In one of my first days at school, I was walking home along the railroad tracks. Those tracks went alongside our house on South Ann and East Bay Streets. I was walking with a few friends. There was an orange orchard to the left surrounded with a barbed wire fence. We noticed a small hole toward the ground that we could easily crawl under. Quick approval from my friends Janie and Susan meant we would make a dash under the fence, grab a few oranges, and run back to the tracks, and no one would be the wiser. We did not count on a big black lab dog that noticed us and made a dash toward us. We didn't get the oranges and quickly turned around and crawled back under the fence. We were so scared that when my shoe fell off due to my foot being too small, I dared not go back to get it. I continued home with one shoe thinking no one would notice.

When I got home, Mom was busy hanging clothes on the line, so I quickly took my one shoe and hid it under the club chair. I went to the bedroom to change into my play clothes. "I'm gonna go to the park and play with Janie," I hollered. I wasn't there but a few minutes when I heard Mom yelling from our backyard toward the park, "ROSALINDAAAAAAA!" Oops, I knew I was in trouble. I rushed home, innocently walking in the front door. Mom, being the clean freak that she had to be with six children, was sweeping the living room with the club chair in the middle of the living room. "Where is your other shoe, *cabrona*?" Get it and take them to the room. Without hesitating, I replied, "Oh, the other shoe, I let Janie borrow it." "What? Why would Janie want to borrow one shoe?" my Mom yelled, with her jugular vein about to explode. "Go get your other shoe right now!" Knowing this was a down-and-out lie, I went outside and sat on the porch, hoping Mom would get back to her cleaning and forget about that dumb shoe. What was so important about a silly pink shoe? They were too big for me anyway.

When she noticed that I was sitting outside without a care to the world, she went to the phone and dialed Ms. Martinez. "Hello, Erlinda? Sorry to bother you, but Rosie says Janie borrowed her pink loafer. Would you know anything about it?" Abruptly, Janie was called in from playing at the park across the street. "Janie, do you have Rosie's shoe? Clara is looking for it. Rosie told her you have it. Do you?" her mother asked. "What? I don't have her shoe. I don't know where it is," cried Janie. Janie didn't want to tell on me so I wouldn't get in trouble, so she evaded details about the lost pink shoe. My mother lost her patience and hung up the phone. She ran outside, grabbed me by my ear, and said, "I'll go settle this once and for all. Those are the only shoes you have, and I'll be damned if you are gonna give one away!" she continued to rant.

We hurriedly walked the one block to Janie's. Janie had already received a paddling and was sitting outside crying. Erlinda saw Mom huffing mad and quickly came outside. They continued to interrogate both of us, but either of us could come up with the location of the shoe. Janie continued to insist she did not have it and didn't know anything about it. I stuck to my story of Janie having it. After my Mom had had enough, she pretty well concluded that this was not going to resolve the issue. She dragged me home. When we got back, she said, "*Go!* Don't come home until you decide what you did with the other shoe. So when you go, you had better find that shoe before your father gets home." Oh no! That was the worst. You never wanted to hear her say, "Wait until your father gets home." That was the ultimate punishment.

I walked toward the railroad tracks in tears back toward Market Street. The older kids were now coming home. Three teens saw me sitting on the tracks in tears and asked, "Why are you crying, Rosie?" I sobbingly replied, "I lost my shoe, and Momma won't let me go home until I find it." One of the older girls asked where I had lost it. Not wanting to reveal we were stealing oranges, I told her a dog had run after me, it had slipped off, and the dog had taken it. "Where was the dog?" Julie asked. "Over there, across from the Butane Man's house, Mr. Garrett," I replied. "Let's go back, and maybe we can find it along the tracks," Julie offered. She grabbed my hand, and we returned to the scene of the crime, and indeed, Julie did find it. It was dangling on one of the lower rungs of the wire fence. Now how did it get there? I'll never tell.

As grown-ups, when we have our holiday family reunions, I'll admit to the lost shoe epic and laugh until I pee in my pants of how Janie and I stuck to our story. Occasionally, I will say to Janie, "Remember when I lent you my shoe?" She looks at me and says, "Yeah, I took a beating with the fly swapper for you!" What a silly lie.

During first and second grade, I attended the Sacred Heart Catholic School, where they had four or five German nuns teaching us. It was a long White House-like building with three rooms, three entrances, and a set of boys' and girls' bathrooms next to the middle room. In the first room were the first and second graders, taught by Sister Anna Maria. At the back right side of the first room was a door with a small hallway leading to the restrooms. At the end of the hall, the door on the left led into the third- and fourth-grade room, taught by Sister Hildegarde. I don't remember if there was an inside entry to the fifth- and sixth-grade room as I never got to go in that room. Sister Petatis was a mean Mother Superior, and I stayed as far away from her as I could. At noon, we would all take our sack lunches with the nuns and sit under the big tree and benches that were built around the huge oak tree. I always made sure I was as far away as possible from Mother Superior.

I only went to Catholic school for two years. I was a lefty, and in those days, they didn't approve of that. Every time I would raise my left hand or pick up my pencil with my left hand, here came Sister Anna Maria with the little wooden ruler to spank my fingers. If I had to go to the bathroom and raised my left hand, I would be ignored, or if I knew the answer to a question, which was highly unlikely, I, again, would get ignored. So finally I didn't want to go to school anymore and would cry in the mornings because I didn't like school. I didn't know how to explain the reason why, so Mom and Dad just thought I was a bad seed and took me out and put me in public school. I was so excited to be free finally. It was a bigger school, and most of my neighborhood friends went there.

At home, it was a race to get dressed in the morning since we only had one tiny bath and a bunch of kids getting ready for school. We all had to get clean teeth and clean hand approval from dad, take our daily vitamin, and drink our juice before eating our break-fast, usually cream-o-wheat, oatmeal, or just a five-cent Little Debbie cake. We all competed on getting a breakfast spot at the kitchen table and riding shotgun in the Picton's flatbed truck Dad used to take us to school. On sunny days, whichever one of us didn't fit in the front would have to ride holding on to the rear window grill on the back of the truck. On cold or rainy days, we just piled in on top of each other the few blocks to school. Since the Catholic school was close by and along the tracks, we used to follow the rails home. However, when we started public school, that was a little farther, so most of the time, we had to be picked up.

Mom didn't drive but was forced to learn. Sometimes, we would rather walk when we saw her coming. She was four foot, eight inches short; the steering column was higher than her, so she used the space in the middle of the wheel to see. She would stick out her hand, usu-ally with a Camel cigarette in between two fingers, or use the blinker at least three blocks or more before she had to make a turn. When she had to use both hands to steer, a Camel was always hanging down the side of her mouth. How she carried a conversation with that thing in her mouth without dropping still baffles me.

That first year of public school was a whole new world. I met kids my age who lived in my neighborhood but down at the other end of Mathis Street, past the park I usually played at. These girls became my buds: Susanna, Magdalena, and Oralia. We did everything together from eating our tortilla taco lunches behind the school building, walking home together, to meeting at the park after school to play. By the end of the third grade, most of us were eight or almost nine years old, and friends at that age were important. I had built a circle of friends. We were looking forward to spending our summer at the beach together.

In May of 1958, the first Sunday after the last day of school, we were all at the beach. It was supposed to be a beautiful sunny day. All our parents were there, and we played in the water. We got separated as I heard someone call my name. When I turned back to find my friends, Susanna, Magdalena, and Oralia were gone. After a frantic search, it was discovered that all three had been pulled under by a riptide. They all drowned. A total of ten beachgoers died that day in those waters, including a visiting priest. It was a sorrowful summer. After that, I could no longer go in the beach waters, at least not past where I could still see my feet. To go any deeper would cause too much anxiety, even to this day. I never learned to swim for this reason.

Nowadays, not much is said of that day. No one talks about it like it was a bad dream. However, I never forgot. I'm reminded of the tragedy all the time. So now I'm home again. I can help my mom, see some old friends, and visit the old haunts. It is good to be back in Rockport for more than a weekend. Yes, coming home is a happy time, but it is also bittersweet.

Rudy Nava with army buddies, Camp Chaffee, Arkansas, 1946.

(L-to-R) Yolli, Rudy, and Clara Nava, 1946.

1945 wartime photo of Rudy Nava that hung in
the home of his mother, Medarda Nava.

Two Sons Home From Battlefronts

Two sons of Mrs. Gregoria Solis
have returned from European bat-
tlefronts and are in Rockport together on furlough.

Tech. Sgt. Sam Solis, son of Mr.
and Mrs. Solis, is on 30-day leave
after being returned to the United
States from France. He has been
overseas with the Army Air Corps
since Oct. 1944. Solis holds the Air
Medal and several other decora-
tions.

Pfc. Cecilio R. Nava is visiting
his wife, daughter and mother here.
He had been overseas with the
Infantry six months and holds two
combat stars. He will report to an
Arkansas station.

Newspaper announcement of Rudy Nava's return from WWII.

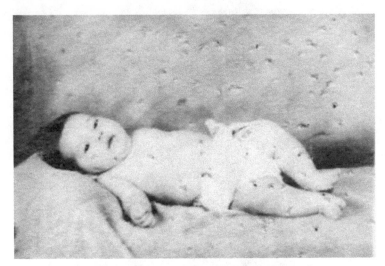

Yolanda "Yolli" Nava, three months old, 1945.

Eugenio Nava holding Eddie Solis (son of MaLala's
sister, Virginia Solis) and Yolanda Nava, 1946.

Tia Tencha's house at 119 N. Pearl Street, across
from Sacred Heart Church in Rockport.

Tia Tencha holding a young Norma Nava, 1952.
Picture taken at the new home of Rudy and Clara Nava,
E. Bay Street at S. Ann Street, Rockport.

Rudy Nava Jr. "Baby Boy," age four, enjoying
the waters of Rockport Beach, 1951.

(L-to-R) Yolanda, Rudy Jr., Rosa, and Nelda Nava
enjoying Easter Sunday, 1952. The tracks on Ann Street
can be seen in the background, on the right.

NEW LIONS NOW ROAR

Rudy Nava, charter president (left) is shown here as he received the charter of the newly-formed club from Charles Seecord, Governor of Lions' District 283, at a dinner meeting held by the club in the Rockport Elementary School Cafeteria recently.

Rudy Nava on the occasion of officially forming the
Lions Club of Rockport, 1964 or 1965.

Group photo of the members of the Rockport
Lions Club from around 1964 or 1965.

Rudy and Clara Nava, early 1960s.

Yolanda's birthday party, with (L-to-R) Rudy Jr. "Baby Boy,"
Aunt Gloria Garcia, Nelda, Hector, and Rosa, 1950s.

Nelda Nava, 1950s.

Rosa Nava enjoying Rockport Beach, 1951.

Hector Nava, early 1950s.

La Banderita

As remembered by Rosa N. Krinsky

Back in the late '20s, possibly even the late '30s, before the Rockport neighborhood of Oak Terrace was developed, there existed way back in the woods a jacal with a flag on a pole. A jacal is an old hut, similar to the adobe-style Native American structures. Well, they called that flagpole La Banderita ("little flag"). Next to this old jacal was a cistern or some type of watering hole where many of the women would go to do their laundry. I believe there was also some type of slaughterhouse nearby. The menfolk would often tell their wives that they were going to take a walk to La Banderita to smoke their Bulgar. The women knew they were going to "eye" the women washing their clothes and do their usual men-talk. When Dad got upset at life, us, or Mom, he always repeated the phrase, "Me voy a ir a La Banderita" ("I'm going to go to the Little Flag"). That place has long been razed and developed into Oak Terrace, but Dad had never forgotten that place. He often still repeated, "Me voy a ir a La Banderita." Occasionally, he'd request to be buried there. Sometimes, if he felt he was too much for us to handle, he'd ask us to "take him to La Banderita" for some peace.

The Cove Drive-In

As remembered by Rosa N. Krinsky

Near the intersection of Texas Highway 35 and Loop 70 sat the Cove Drive-In. On Thursday night, admission was one dollar for each car-load to watch a movie. We would look for someone with a pickup, usually Stella Perez, and promise to pay her way, and then everyone in the neighborhood would go in the bed of her truck. Once we got to the drive-in, we would all jump out and head for the concession stand. There were two rows of benches in front, so we mostly sat out there to meet our buddies or kept our fingers crossed that a special someone would sit next to us to possibly steal a kiss or two. Boys back then didn't have an allowance to buy us chicks a Coke or pop-corn, just the quarter their parents would give them. The boys usu-ally climbed over the fence and snuck in for free. They always shared their popcorn and would undoubtedly offer you a stick of their Juicy Fruit gum.

Originally built in 1953, a storm irreparably damaged the Cove Drive-In in the early 1980s. The money needed to replace the equip-ment and repair the building wasn't deemed worth it, and the locale was shuttered forever. The old lot is near present-day 401 Tenth Street. I believe part of the old lot now belongs to a boat and RV storage company.

The Dances

As remembered by Rosa N. Krinsky

Back in the 1950s and 1960s, dances were the common source of entertainment. Every Sunday night, there was a dance at Bonnie & Doug's in Aransas Pass for one dollar. Then on Monday nights, Domingo Pena held dances at the Exposition Hall in Corpus Christi. These were five dollars because there were always many opening bands before the headliner band. I don't know how we did it, but we would try to go every other Monday night.

We would save our lunch money by not eating, taking our lunch, or making it through the day on a five-cent Coke and a five-cent bag of chips. If we felt like splurging, we would get a five-cent Coke and an order of fries for fifteen cents, but mostly just chips. We needed two weeks to save the money for Domingo Pena's dances on Monday. Nelda and I always worked, either at Mary's Malt or washing dishes for a weekend tourist. We would get home around 2 a.m. from the dances, but we dared not complain; otherwise, Mom and Dad would not take us anymore. We always went with them when we wanted to go dancing in Corpus. We were not allowed to go "out of town" on our own. Besides, Mom and Dad also liked to dance. They would go with another couple; Dad would drink a few Falstaffs, and Mom would down a few Tom Collins because they knew that I would be the designated driver.

When we went to Bonnie & Doug's on Sunday nights, even though it was in Aransas Pass, Dad would let us take his car as long as an adult drove. We would pay Stella's way, and she would drive us, along with our entire entourage, which included Lizzie, Kitty,

Pauline, Ginny, Julia, Ida, Irma, myself, and my sisters, Nelda and Norma. We also all had to chip-in a nickel for gas. Yep, we all made ourselves fit into that 1961 Ford Fairlane!

Another place Mom and Dad would take us was Bonnie View. It was a very, very small cotton-pickin' community, mainly ranches, where dances were held for the cotton pickers on Saturday nights. Again, Mom and Dad would take another couple, and I would go as the designated driver. Dad had his rules regarding his daughters going to too many dances. There was a prerequisite that if we went to a dance on a Saturday night, we must agree to go to church the following day. No exceptions. The same went for going out with our friends to the beach, just cruising, or to the dance on Sunday night. If you couldn't go to church on Sunday morning, no way you were going anywhere that Sunday night. We always went to church, and certainly on our best behavior.

If it so happened that we had gone to Bonnie & Doug's the Sunday before, it was forbidden for us to ask to go the following week again since we were only allowed to go dancing every two weeks since dances in Aransas Pass and Corpus Christi were always on school nights.

Sometimes, we would make plans among our friends to talk my dad into letting us go. Our friends would come over, butter my dad up, help in the yard, help us clean our room, and be good girls. We would sit in our room curling our hair and picking out what we would wear. When the girls would leave to get themselves ready, Nelda and I would begin our pleading. First, we would shower and tell our parents we were getting ready for the next day to beat the rush in the bathroom later in the night. We would quietly put on our nylons and house slippers, our undergarments, full slips, and then our robe. We would sit around in the living room, joking and just being good. After a while, when we felt Dad was jolly enough, we would break it to him with our appeal to "please let us go to Bonnie & Doug's in Aransas Pass to the dance." His usual response was, "Didn't you go dancing last weekend?"

"Si, señor."

"Then don't bother asking. You know the rules," he would harp back.

"But, Daddy, Ricky G. is playing, and all the girls need a ride, and if we don't take them, then no one can go. Please?" We'd implore with tears in our eyes.

"I said *no*, and that's it. Now go to your room and go *steady*."

To our dismay, he meant "go study," but his Mexican tongue would pronounce the *u* like "ea." We would reply jokingly, "Let us go dancing, and we'll find someone to go 'steady' with!" With that, off we went, shuffling our slippered feet. We would wait a few minutes and return sad faced and again ask, "Please, Daddy? We promise to put gas in the car!"

"*No*! Now that's final," he would always answer. "Go to your room, and I don't want to hear it again!"

Off we went, this time making tearful cries, fake as they were. In between sobs, we would say things like, "You're so strict. That's why no one likes us" or "I'm going to make an F on my science test just for that!" Then we would slip in a plea of "Pleaseeeeeeeee, Daddy?"

After that, we would quiet down. We could hear Mom begging Dad to let us go, listing the millions of reasons why we deserved it. We kept our grades up, most of the time; cleaned the entire house once a week; and kept our room clean every day. While sitting on pins and needles, we would hear Dad walk towards our room and slowly open the door. We put on a sad face, looking up at him with our sad faces,

"Yes, sir?"

"What time does it start?"

"Nine," we'd reply in unison.

"I'm gonna let you go this time, but only if you can get Stella to drive. Take my car, replace the gas you use, and be home by 2:00 a.m. because tomorrow is school. If I hear one word of anyone being tired or doesn't want to get up, that will be the last time you go out on a school nigh

"Yes, sir," we'd sing out.

The minute he walked out of our room, we yanked rollers out of our hair, tore the robe off, and slipped on our shifts (dresses that were in style in the early '60s), and within five minutes, we were out the door. Of course, our entourage had kept calling every five minutes to see if we were close to a yes, so they too were ready. Nelda, Norma, and I would drive our 1961 Ford Fairlane to Stella's down the block and pile in Lizzie, Kitty, and Pauline. Pauline would sometimes drive with Arnold, her beau, and that meant more room. Then we'd go around the next block to pick up my two cousins, Ginny and Julia. Then off to the other neighborhood to pick up Ida and Irma. We charged them twenty-five cents each since they were kind of out of our way.

Between Ginny and Julia chipping in ten cents each, Stella and her girls would ride for free since Stella was the driver. That would give us seventy cents for gas. Gas was twenty-four cents a gallon. Aransas Pass was nine miles away, so we would travel twenty miles total and put in 2 1/2 gallons of gas. Not bad. Dad would earn at least one gallon or more of gas for the privilege of allowing us to use the car. That was about how we calculated it. Once we got to Bonnie and Doug's, we would put the same three tables together with Stella sitting in the middle chair. The rest of us girls would sit around her. She was like a mother hen with us.

If it were a special occasion, since I liked to sew, I would make a custom shift dress for Ginny, Julia, my sisters Nelda and Norma, and myself. Shifts were quick to make, and I usually just changed the necklines to make each unique. However, the fabric was all the same. I would add a V-shape kerchief to wear on our hair if it was a daytime event. We would go on Saturdays and find lovely fabric at Spark's Sporting Goods on Austin Street. We would put our fabrics on layaway, putting down twenty-five cents a week until we paid it off.

After the dance, we had to go to Little Bobs. Dad had allowed us time before our curfew to do this. We would all order a big platter of french fries and gravy and a glass of iced tea. We would share the platter of fries, but we each had our own tea. By the time we took all the girls home, we would barely make curfew. It was a must that we wake Dad to announce our arrival so he could check if we had broken curfew. Since I was driving home after we dropped Stella and the girls off, I often asked Nelda to go inside and tell Dad we were home while I put the car in the garage. If we had cut it too close, smarty Nelda, knowing darn well we had missed curfew by a few minutes, would sometimes make it worse by going directly to the bathroom and locking herself in. By the time I came in, I had assumed she had already told Dad, so I would go to our room and commence to get undressed. After enough time had gone by and Dad would wake up from hearing us, Nelda would finally come out of the bathroom like everything was okay. When I asked if she told Dad that we were home, she would shyly reply, "No, I thought you did." Since I was the oldest, Dad blamed me. I got the lecture, while Nelda and Norma calmly went to bed, leaving me to answer Dad's questions through their closed bedroom door. I'm sure they could hear me, "Si, señor," "No, señor," "Si, señor," "Hasta mañana!" As I got in bed, I would read Nelda the riot act but nary a care she had. We slept in one big bed, the three of us. Norma was in the middle and Nelda and me on either side. When I was mad at Nelda, I wouldn't let her rub her feet against mine to get warm. That was her punishment for getting us in trouble. It was always Nelda's fault. She liked the lead singer of the band and could hardly pry herself away from him after the dances. I love my sister, but sometimes, I think she enjoyed getting us in trouble!

Clara Nava, 1967.

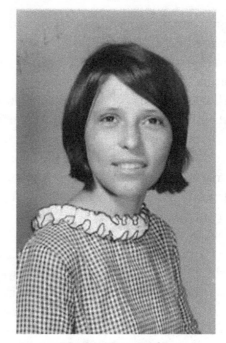

Norma Nava, 1965.

Rosa Nava, 1966.

Rudy Nava Jr, 1966.

(L-to-R) Linda Taylor, Sheryl, Maxine Leet, Rosa Nava, 1961.

Rudy's Moneymaker

As remembered by Rosa N. Krinsky

When he was ten years old, Dad got himself a little job working for Ms. Bracht, no relation to the local business owners. Ms. Bracht was from San Antonio and usually only came to Rockport on weekends and holidays. Young Rudy Nava expressed an eagerness to work in exchange for whatever little spending money he could make. She didn't need any help around the home, but instead of just offering a handout, she encouraged his work ethic and decided to hire him.

Like most people in Rockport and most dry areas of Texas, Ms. Bracht's yard was full of those annual summer nuisances called grass burrs, or sticker burrs. It's a type of weed that spreads in dry, sandy soil and produces those annoying sharp, barbed burrs. They are painful and, as you can imagine, difficult to remove from clothing. Well, Ms. Bracht decided to hire Rudy to pull these little prickly bothersome burrs from her yard. Rudy was proud to oblige. He carried his trusty dinner fork in his back pocket every day as he walked by the home in hopes she would need his services. He would even go by during the week, after school, to see if she was in town. If she were, he would knock on the door. If she were home, she would often accept his gracious offer, and he'd get to work. He would pull out his trusty fork or, as he called it, his "moneymaker," get on his knees, and start to clear the yard of as many burrs as he could. He would jab the fork into the soil, and the weeds would get lodged in between the tines, or prongs, of the fork. He would then pull them up, as many as he could, for about an hour or so until he had to get home for dinner.

This was back around 1936, and Rudy earned about fifty cents for his work, which at the time was pretty good spending money for a child. As of 2008, Ms. Bracht's old house still stood there on the corner of Concho and Magnolia Street.

Puppy Love

by Rudy Nava, at the age of eighty-two years
(as told to Rosa Nava Krinsky, November 2007)

When I was twelve or thirteen years old, I would get out of school, which was on Live Oak Street, and walk back one block to Nopal Street and up one block to Magnolia Street, where just the white people lived. There on the left corner was the house of the prettiest girl in Rockport. Her name was Mary Virginia Jackson, a name I shall never forget. Most of the time, she would be sitting on a rocking chair on her veranda with her legs crossed. She had the prettiest legs I had ever seen, although I had not seen too many. As I passed her house, my head would look straight ahead, but my eyes would be looking toward her, trying to steal a glimpse. I would pass her house, then turn around and slowly stroll back and look at her again. After I had my fill of what I believed to be the picture of perfection, I would rush home, hoping not to be too late. I did this every day after school in hopes that she would be sitting on her porch. She didn't know who I was and never noticed my daily ritual.

Cecilio Rodolfo Mondragon's Namesake

As remembered by Rosa N. Krinsky

When Medarda Nava was in her twenties, she was keeping company, colloquial-speak for dating, with an older Mexican gentleman by the name of Cecilio Rodolfo Mondragon. Medarda's mother, Maria de Jesus, died in February 1925 when Medarda was twenty-four years old and still unmarried. So she wouldn't be alone with her father, Eugenio, she went to live with her baby sister, Hortencia. Hortencia, or Tencha as she was known, had been married for a few months to a man named Gavino Garza. They lived just down the street on Cornwall. Less than a year later, Medarda gave birth to a son, whom she named Cecilio Rodolfo, after her boyfriend, although, she always called him Rodolfo. Medarda and her new son went back home to live with her father, Eugenio, who still lived alone on the family homestead off Cornwall and Highway 35. When Cecilio was two years old, Medarda and her boyfriend, Cecilio Mondragon, got married in Aransas County. The couple and child moved to Victoria, Texas. There, she called back home often, telling of being mistreated by her new husband. After being severely beaten one day, she called her father, Eugenio, to pick her and young Rodolfo up. By 1930, she was again living with her father and three-year-old son in the family home in Rockport. She never legally changed her name to her husband's surname of Mondragon. Rodolfo lived his life using her maiden name of Nava as his surname just as Medarda did. Medarda lived the rest of her life and died, never again uttering any mention of her marriage to Cecilio Rodolfo Mondragon. She had only the memory, her old marriage license, a solitaire amethyst ring, and her namesake son to remember him by. Interestingly enough, Medarda was never legally divorced from Mondragon.

An Afternoon Snack for Rudy and Chavela

As related to Rosa Nava Krinsky

When Rudy and his first cousin Isabel Solis, or Chavela as she was known, would come home from school, it was a must to pass by their Tia Tencha's house. Tia Tencha had a big brood, so it was imperative for her to start her large batch of tortillas early for supper. Tia Tencha would put the already-made hot homemade tortillas in a basket and hang the basket with a pulley rope from the ceiling. She would say it was to keep the bugs and vermin away, but I genuinely believe it was to keep the kids from eating before dinner. Chavela and Rudy would come in the back door, quickly pull down the basket, and grab a few tortillas and continue on their merry way home, all the while enjoying their rolled-up hot tortillas. Tio Gavino always knew what they were doing, but he just sat at the back of the house, smoking, never saying a word. Tia Tencha was too busy with the housework to notice them taking their afternoon snack.

Fresh Corn Tortillas

As remembered by Rosa Nava Krinsky

Back in the early 1950s, during the summers, I would stay with my grandmother, Longina Muñoz, in Alice, Texas. Since my *madrina* lived in the same barrio, actually not far away, I was allowed to walk over there to watch my Tia/Madrina Rafaelita Muñoz and Tio Paz Herrera make fresh corn tortillas in their *molino*.[92] When I say making fresh corn tortillas, I mean homemade real corn tortillas, with freshly ground corn *masa*. Nowadays, fresh corn tortillas mean buying corn flour from the supermarket and using dehydrated *masa*, like Maseca. It's common these days to use this modern method when making tortillas, tamales, and quesadillas. So while this type of *masa harina* does indeed produce some tasty food, it doesn't compare to the texture and flavor of what my Tia Rafaelita would make! I was very young, but I can still vaguely remember my Tio Paz going down the street in his horse-drawn wagon calling out, "Tortillas! Tortillas! Calientes! Recien hechas!" He would come ringing a bell signaling to all that the tortillas were ready. It would be every day around 11:00 a.m. or noon so the workmen could have hot tortillas when they came home for lunch. If I was at *Buelita's*,[93] I would run outside and grab one of Tio Paz's prewrapped, in butcher paper, stacks of tortillas and bring them inside. Then I would go back out front and wait for my three uncles, Ramiro, Enrique Jr., and Israel Muñoz, to come home for lunch. They all worked for the nearby Coca-Cola plant and would come home driving the big delivery trucks (at least they looked big to me). I used to enjoy playing on the trucks and sneaking away a few small bottles of Coke to drink later. I remember back then many household items were delivered fresh directly to your home, like tortillas, milk, and yummy *pan dulce*![94]

I used to love visiting *mi abuelita*! Besides the smell of fresh tortillas, I remember that bell my Tio Paz used to ring every day because my mother inherited it from one of his children, her cousins. That bell always meant family and fresh tortillas!

Rockport's Darkest Day

A Recollection by Rosa Nava Krinsky

When I was a young girl, I was not only present when three of my best friends tragically drowned, but I came very close to being a victim myself. It all occurred at the Rockport Beach in 1958. I was reading an article about the fiftieth anniversary of the tragic event written by Norma Martinez, which was published in the May 24, 2008, issue of *The Rockport Pilot*. It all came back to me so vividly—the emotions, the sadness. A total of seven people drowned that horrible day after my friends roamed into unmarked deep water created by recent sand dredging near the beach. Those who drowned were Susana Virginia Torres, 9; Margarita Torres, 11; Oralia Cruz Tamez, 10; Dave W. Curby, 6; Mary Bailey, and her daughter, Janice, 9; and Father Leonard Berry, 40.

It was May of 1958, just a few months before I was going to turn nine years old. What should have been a happy occasion, playing in the surf with my friends, ended up being a devastating tragedy that would impact me forever. It is difficult to recall the precise story as I was very young. Over the years, when I would ask for details from my peers, parents, grandparents, and young teens who witnessed the event, no one remembered, or instead refused to remember. Surely, I thought, *I wasn't the only one there! I still remember it! How could I ever forget?*

Granted, many may have just erased this tragedy from their minds as if it never happened. After all, it was so many years ago, but the memory keeps barging into my head many times every day, quick flashes of detail as though it were only yesterday.

Many families were affected, and many, many more were touched. My three best friends, classmates, and neighbors were suddenly gone forever—a situation an innocent eight-year-old could not understand. It meant being alone as I was that summer with not one friend in the world. They had gone to another life, another world, all together, to run, play, and be happy without me. I kept asking myself, "What had I done wrong that I was not taken with them?" or "What had I done right that I was still here, breathing, living, and existing?" Now fifty-nine years later, I still remember the lives of my three best friends, Susana, Margarita, and Oralia. I want you to remember them too.

After I attended Sacred Heart Catholic School, it was to be my first year of public school. It was a whole new world. I met kids my age who lived in my neighborhood. They lived down at the other end of Mathis Street, past Spencer Park, where I usually played. These girls became my best buds, Susana Torres, her older cousin, Margarita Torres, and a new girl to the neighborhood, Oralia Tamez. We did everything together, from eating our tortilla taco lunches behind the school building to walking home in a group and playing at the park after school. By the end of the third grade, most of us were eight or almost nine years old, and at that age, having close friends was very important. I had built my circle of friends and so looked forward to spending our summer at the beach together.

It was the first Sunday after the last day of school in May 1958. It was to be a beautiful sunny day, and we had all planned to meet at the beach. Most parents always went, parking their cars at the water's edge from where they watched the children play in knee-deep water. That particular Sunday, Susana, Oralia, and I were playing in the water on tire tubes, while another group was splashing and playing pop the whip. Everyone was having a good time. In a faint distance, I could hear my name called from ashore. It was Pat and Sue Clark, shouting, "Rosie, Rosie, wait for us." I turned and started to walk toward shore to meet them. As we returned to the other girls, I lost my direction and stopped to look around. I couldn't see Susana or Oralia anywhere. The beach was crowded since it was the first weekend of the summer break. I walked in several directions looking for them, but they were nowhere to be found. I assumed they had followed me. We returned to shore to continue to look for them. When we didn't see them, I found Oralia's father, Mr. Tamez. "Where's Oralia?" I asked.

"Isn't she with you?" he replied.

"Oh yeah," I said frightenedly, "but I came to get my friends, and when I went back to her and Susana, I couldn't find them. Maybe she just drifted toward another direction."

We went back to the water, yelling for Susana, Oralia, and Margarita. Occasionally, we would stop and play in hopes that they would eventually find us. Suddenly, Mr. Tamez appeared, still looking for Oralia. We told him we still didn't know where she was.

Now panicking, Mr. Tamez began to yell for her. He rushed ashore to be sure she wasn't sleeping in the car or collecting shells along the shore. He asked other parents if she were with their children. Alarmed, other parents began looking for their children as well.

Mr. Tamez returned to the water screaming, "Oraliaaaaaa, Oraliaaaaa," but to no avail. Soon, other adults began the same routine, yelling and asking others close by if they had seen their children. Mothers suddenly started holding on to their children in relief as they returned after being called.

Suddenly, it was not a beautiful day anymore. The sky became dark as though a large blanket had been laid across the sky. Mr. Tamez was still in the water, still trying to find Oralia. Suddenly, a boy from our neighborhood, Joe Martinez, saw Mr. Tamez struggling to stay afloat even though the water was not over his chest. He was a good swimmer, so I surmised that a big fish or shark must have caught him. I started praying, thinking that it could even be the end of the world. How could this be happening?

Panic quickly set in among the parents. Joe ran into the water and had a difficult time from being pulled under by a powerful undercurrent. He fell inside a deep hole but managed to pull himself out and even grabbed Mr. Tamez, bringing him ashore.

Mr. Tamez had swallowed quite a bit of water and was out of breath. He was physically and emotionally exhausted. After he caught his breath, he knew the lost children had been caught in the same hole and current that almost took his life.

Very soon, all the compadres, the men who had boats, brought them to the area. They formed a circle utilizing six big shrimp boats and began dredging with nets to see if they could somehow catch whatever was causing this mysterious panic.

The skies turned dark, and a hush fell over the beach. No one seemed to be moving. Several families were huddled close and praying that their loved one would be found. I only knew of my three friends—Susana, Margarita, and Oralia—who were missing. As we watched the shrimp boats dredging the nets and occasionally picking up their anchors, we prayed we would not see the inevitable.

All of a sudden, the world seemed to stop. One boat pulled in its anchor with something hooked to it. "What was it?" everyone wondered aloud. I was in the family car by then, and my mother pushed us down on the floorboard. She didn't want us to see what she feared was going to be pulled up. I was determined to look because it was my friends who were lost. As I stared at the object, I prayed it wasn't Susana, Oralia, or Margarita. The other boats began to pull in their nets, and their catch was sickening. Screams and cries could be heard from the moms and dads that were watching from ashore.

It seemed like an eternity before it was all over, with the dark haze still hovering over the beach. There were a total of ten pulled from the deep water that afternoon, seven of whom had drowned. Among the drowned were my missing three best friends as well as a visiting priest and some tourists from out of town.

I began to sob uncontrollably. Was I selfish? All I could think of was who my friends would be when school starts in September. Did I not deserve good friends? Why would God take these good people away from me and leave me all alone? My priorities were not in order, but I was just a child of eight. I would ponder these thoughts for many, many years.

In the 1950s, funeral homes were too expensive, so bodies were viewed in homes. All the furniture was moved out of the tiny front room of the Tamez house to accommodate three little coffins. Oralia was in the middle, with Susana and Margarita on each side. They looked like little angels sleeping. They were all dressed in their white Holy Communion dresses with their rosaries and Bibles in their cupped hands. Every night, I would wear my Sunday best, walk down one block to the house for the viewing, sit on the floor less than two feet from the coffins, and say the rosary with the other "Sodality Girls" from our church. It was a week I shall never forget.

It was a lonely summer, and when September came around, I was lost. My memories of my friends were still so vivid that I could not function. I would have nightmares during the night and wake up screaming. I would see images of nets or anchors with bodies in them. Mom would take me to *curanderas*[95] for spiritual healings. A neighbor, Doña Elvira Falcon, would run a broom across my body in a sweeping motion while I was covered with a white sheet from head to toe, all the while in prayer. She would hold an uncracked egg and wave it over my body to extract the evil in me. Later, she would crack the egg and place it in a glass under the bed for the bad spirit to exit. A day later, she would look at it and either say, "It worked," or "We need to do it again."

Some years back, I was contacted by David Bailey, the son of Mary Bailey and brother of Janice Bailey, who both perished that tragic day. David was only two years old when he lost his mother and sister. He is living in South Carolina and is doing well. His mother and sister are buried in the Rockport Cemetery. We talked briefly and caught up. We had hoped to stay in touch, but unfortunately, you know how things go. We haven't spoken since, but we are Facebook friends.

Occasionally, now in my retirement years, I will go into the cemetery where all three of my childhood friends are buried side by side. It reminds me that had Pat and Sue Clark not called for me to come to them on shore, I too would have met my fate that day. It's a sobering thought, one that I will never forget.

My Childhood Visits to Rockport

As remembered by Randy Krinsky

Though I was born in New York, Texas has been my home for most of my life. When I was growing up, most of my summer vacations and many holidays were spent in my mother's hometown of Rockport. We'd go for birthdays, weddings, parties, you name it. Rockport was such a picturesque town to me—tranquil, scenic, and refreshing to the senses.

As a child, you could forgive me for thinking that fresh seafood was an everyday food. My family in Rockport served it so readily and often that it wasn't until I was quite older that I realized it could be pretty pricey! However, we never worried about that when I was younger. Anytime my mother drove my sister and me down Highway 35 to Rockport, my grandmother, or one of my aunts, always had a steaming pot of boiled shrimp waiting for us and then fried red snapper and fried shrimp for dinner. My Uncle Hector and my Uncle Lito were shrimp boat captains, and it seemed they always had an endless supply.

Whether we were there visiting for a wedding, or a holiday, or to spend the weekend with family, it was treated like a big occasion. The family would always gather at my grandparent's home. That was the central meeting place. I remember riding that long trip, four hours back, when the speed limit was 55 mph, and crossing that big bridge on Highway 35 over Copano Bay. Even though we were tired, we were always rejuvenated when we would realize we were getting closer to our destination. We turned off Highway 35 on FM 1069, on down to the West Terrace subdivision, turning south at the

Cracker Barrel, then right at West Terrace Boulevard, then left on Raven Drive, winding our way closer and closer. Our anticipation was building! Finally, we turned that corner on Mallard Drive and hanging a quick left onto Warbler Lane, past Darla Cassel's corner house. If we had been napping or groggy, we were indeed up and alert by now and getting ready to see our family. Finally, we would arrive at 1113 Warbler Lane, where my grandparents lived.

The area was still pretty sparsely populated back then. The whole long block could fit about eight or nine homes but only had four, well really three. About halfway down the street, on the right, was the Rodriguez house, home to Cesar and Lydia, close family friends. Right next door to them was my grandparents' house. Next was "The Shop." That was a two-room building; it looked like a small home, but it was where my grandfather owned a modest side business making window screens. The screen business was one room, which encompassed most of the building due to storage and equipment. The other room was small and looked like a big kitchen. That was used for a seasonal duck-cleaning business; at least it was the few times I was pressed into service. They had me cleaning ducks, defeathering and the like, whenever hunters brought them in to be processed for cooking. It was never really my thing.

Next to that building was the Garcia residence, home to my Uncle Lito and Aunt Yolanda, my mother's eldest sister. That was pretty much it! In my real younger days, no one else lived there on that block.

Visiting was always a joyous occasion. Our grandparents, Rudy and Clara Nava, were always there to greet us with smiles, hugs, and kisses. Before we even arrived, you could see all the cars lined up, parked in front of the house. Even if we weren't coming for a big event, my grandparents always had an ample amount of visitors stopping by to say hello and reminisce.

Walking in, we'd always see my Aunt Yolanda and Uncle Lito, my Uncle Hector and Aunt Frances, and if he was in town, my Uncle Baby Boy and Aunt Emma. Back then, Baby Boy's family lived in Wyoming, before moving to Corpus Christi, before retiring and returning home to Rockport, where he now resides. We called him

Baby Boy because, well, that was just what everyone called him: "the Baby Boy" of the family. That started back before he had a younger brother, Hector, but the name stuck. Everyone, plus friends and neighbors, like Cesar and Lydia Rodriguez, would be over at my grandparents' home visiting. It seemed like such a happy place back then, full of laughter and stories of the old days. Of course, now those stories would be the *really* old days.

Without a doubt, the first thing out of my grandmother's mouth would be, "Are you hungry?" To which we would most assuredly reply, "Yes!" She would head into the kitchen, and my sister and I would hop onto the barstools and stare across the bar as she prepared plates of fried shrimp, mashed potatoes, green beans, and just about anything else she had set up on the counters. If they had tamales earlier that day, she'd look our way with that look in her eye as if to say, "You want some of this too?" We'd nod in the affirmative, and she would pile it on the plate. One thing was for sure: in the Nava house, you never went hungry. She never failed to offer up a platter of *pan dulce*, Mexican sweetbread, when we were all done.

The adults would be sitting at the dining room table across from the kitchen bar. They'd be drinking coffee and nibbling on *pan dulce* while talking about the latest gossip and family affairs. As a child, I never really knew what they were talking about, and I didn't care. I was too focused on that *pan dulce*! After we finished eating, we'd take our plates into the kitchen to wash them in the sink, or I should say, we'd attempt to do so. Grandma would always come in and tell us to leave them there, and she would do it. I don't think she liked the way we cleaned them. Hey, we were kids, and not much about kids was clean.

We'd play outside and visit. One of the first people I'd have to see was the neighbor, Cesar and Lydia's son, Lando. His real name was Orlando Rodriguez, but he was Lando to his friends. Unfortunately, Lando passed away around ten years ago. He was still young, and we, his family and friends, would miss him always. However, back then growing up, he and I were pretty close, and I always visited with him when I was in town. We'd climb trees, listen to music, and explore the thick brush in the fields across and behind my grandparents' home. I had tons of cousins in Rockport. A trip to town always meant hanging out with at least a few of them.

Although, no trip would be complete without walking over a few blocks to Cha Cha Laca Street to see my cousin Joey. He was my mother's cousin, but we were around the same age, had similar interests, and got along great. I even spent a summer once staying with him and his parents, Uncle Daniel and Aunt Gloria, my grandmother's sister. We loved our music, especially Journey and KISS.

Sometimes, my cousins Freddy and Romy would be around. Freddy was my Aunt Nelda's son, while Romy was the son of my Uncle Baby Boy. Both Freddy and Romy were younger than me, as was Lando, but we all got along great and hung out when we could. We'd pop fireworks, climb trees, or wrestle, basically be young boys horseplaying.

In the evenings, when it was dinnertime, we would come in and get cleaned up and ready to eat. We'd gather at either my grandparents' home or down the street at my Aunt Yolanda's house. They would lay out the catch of the day, fried red snapper. Back then, red snapper was the only fish I ever ate. Other than catfish, I don't think I ever ate any different type of fish until I was an adult. While the food was great, I do remember enjoying hearing my grandmother talking about what other family members were up to; not near relatives, but distant relatives. She would always make a point to explain to me who they were and how they were related; basically, almost everyone in Rockport was related to me, whether through blood or marriage.

That was the way it was in Rockport. My family bloodlines ran deep. One afternoon, my grandmother sat down with me and told me about all the relationships that comprised my vast family. I guess I can say that my mother and I got our family history curiosity from my grandmother. As she explained it, our extended family was basically two separate bloodlines: Nava and Flores. This was simplified and didn't take into account older generations, such as the Rodriguez line. She proceeded to tell me about the family of Jose Angel Flores, known as *Don Angel*, or Angelo to family, and his wife, *Doña Consuelo*. *Don Angel* and *Doña Consuelo* had about sixteen or seventeen children. Some of their grandchildren married the sons and daughters of my grandparents. One of their daughters, Stella Flores, is the mother of Uncle Anthony, fathered by my grandfather Rudy Nava Sr. The two families were very close and were neighbors for a time. I might be oversimplifying this, but that was the gist of it.

Let's see, *Don Angel* and *Doña Consuelo* had a daughter, Jovita, known as Joyce. Her first marriage was to a man named Felix Garcia. They had a few children, one of whom was Felix "Lito" Garcia. He married my Aunt Yolanda, my mother's elder sister.

Joyce's sister, Estella, is the aforementioned Stella whom my grandfather pursued in his younger days. Unfortunately for the couple, my great-grandmother, MaLala, had other plans for Grandpa, and he was forced to break it off with Stella. She gave birth to my Uncle Anthony in May 1943. He grew up being friends with his half-sisters and half-brothers but was not publicly accepted as family, out of respect for Stella's husband, Tony Peres. I once saw Uncle Anthony at a party in Rockport. He was the spitting image of my grandfather, and I remember commenting, "Hey, he looks just like Grandpa!" My mother quickly gave me that death stare and pinched me. "Hush! Don't say that," she strongly urged in my ear. She pulled me aside and explained to me that he looked like my grandfather because he was indeed my grandpa's son. I was in my late teens when I learned the truth. All those years, I had another uncle and didn't know it. It was an open secret but one that I wasn't in on. Years later, Tony Peres passed, and in November 2002, Stella passed away as well. Uncle Anthony began to be included in family gatherings and could often be seen on holidays and at family parties surrounded by his Nava brothers and sisters. Sadly, he passed on June 30, 2018.

Joyce and Stella had a younger sister, Elena, called Helen. She married a man named Joe Covarrubias and had four children: Bennie Joe, Gaspar, Michael, and Anthony. Gaspar Covarrubias grew up and married my Aunt Nelda, my mother's younger sister.

Joyce, Stella, and Helen had a baby brother named Guillermo Flores, better known as Willie. Growing up, I always called him Uncle Willie; actually, I still do. He is fun to be around, always quick with a witty remark.

Willie married Elvira Martinez and had five children: Willie Jr., Frances, Terry, Kim, and Vince. In 1976, Frances married my mother's baby brother, Hector.

Whether through blood or marriage, Rockport is all one big family—my family. Though I might not know everyone or get to see as many as I'd like to, we're still family. Those childhood days, when everyone still lived nearby, were some of the happiest memories I have.

No matter what the future holds for our family, we have a rich history and a lot of cherished memories, memories that I hope we pass down to future generations. One of the worst things that can happen to a family is to forget where you came from. I'm hoping that in some small way, my words, as written here in this book, may help in keeping those memories alive.

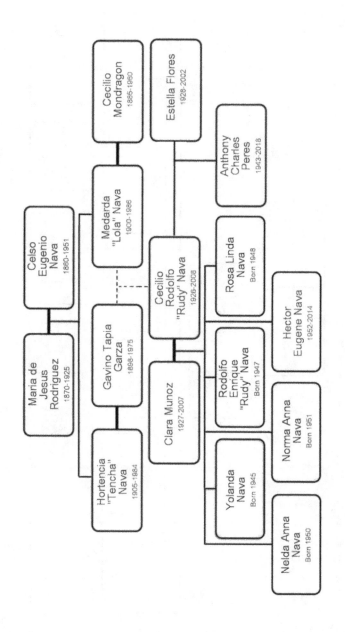

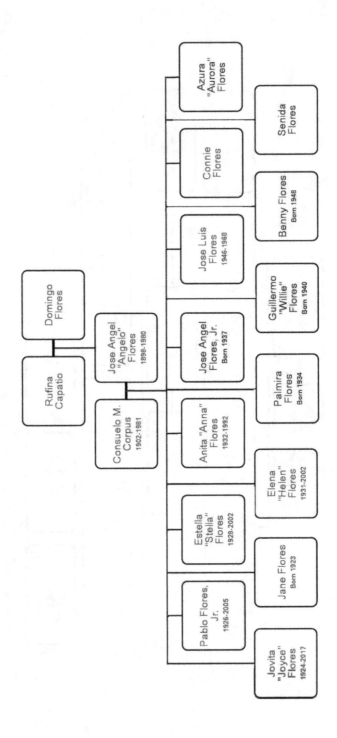

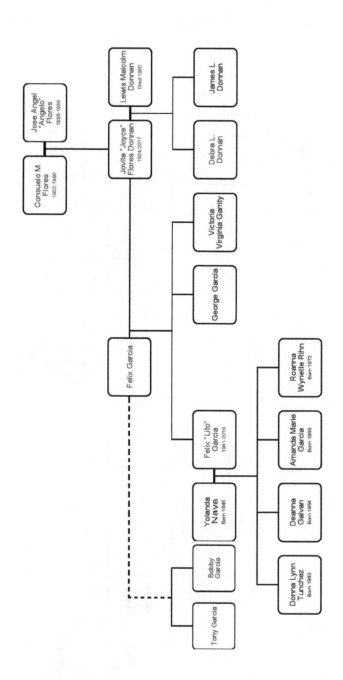

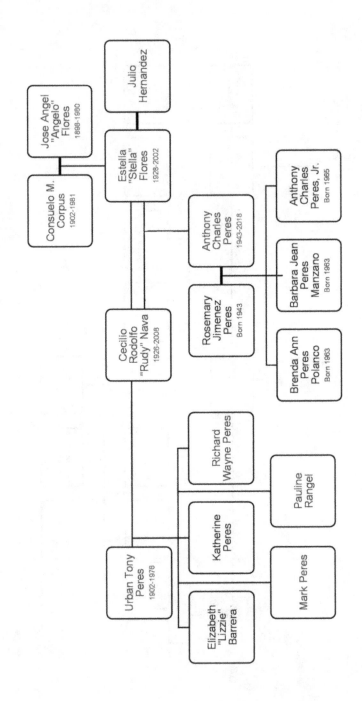

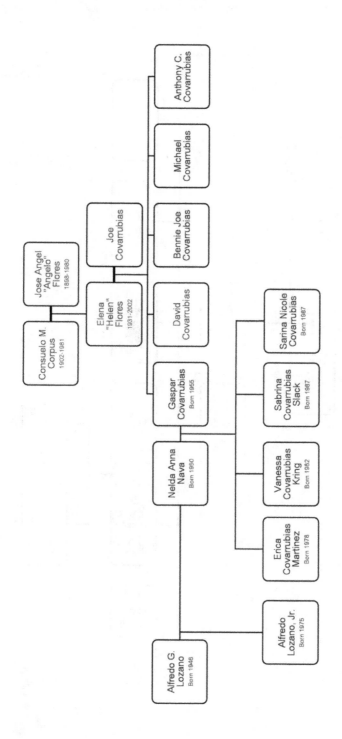

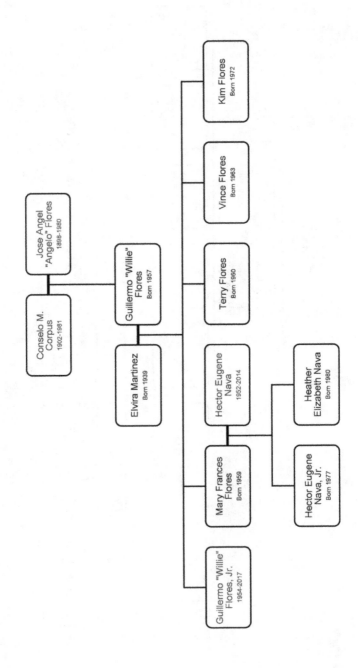

New York City, August 1971: Rosa Nava Krinsky,
Charles Krinsky, and the author, Randy Krinsky.

On a train bound for somewhere, 1972, Rosa Nava
Krinsky and the author, Randy Krinsky.

Rudy Nava with Rosa Nava Krinsky in New York City, 1971.

Rudy Nava with grandson Randy Krinsky, New York City, 1971.

Nava Sisters: Rosa and Nelda, 1972.

Yolanda Nava Garcia, 1963.

Medarda "MaLala" Nava, in her Rockport home, c. early 1980s.

Rudy and Clara Nava's fiftieth wedding anniversary celebration, with most of the grandchildren and great-grandchildren (*L-to-R*): Deanna Garcia Galvan, Hector Nava, Joshua Garcia, Donna Garcia, Jacob Galvan, Roanna Garcia, Rudy Sr., Mandy Garcia, Stefanie Garza, Krystal Isom, Rissa Krinsky, Clara, Longina Munoz (Clara's mother), Timo Galvan, Randy Krinsky, Jason Garza, Sean Garza, Jeatonne Nava, and Heather Nava, Rockport, 1993.

Rudy and Clara Nava, fiftieth wedding anniversary, Rockport, Texas, 1993.

Then: (1992) (*L-to-R*) Randy Krinsky, Joe Garcia, Rick Rinche, and Rissa Krinsky, Nava cousins get together in Houston.

Now: (January 2018) (*L-to-R*) Joe Garcia, Randy Krinsky, Rick Rinche, a little older but still a good-looking group of guys!

Rosa Nava Krinsky with Clara Nava, 1993.

On vacation: Rudy and Clara Nava, 1996.

The Nava siblings with mother, Clara, around the late 1990s
(*L-to-R*): Yolanda, Rosa, Clara, Rudy Jr., Norma, and Nelda.

The Nava siblings with father, Rudy, in the early 2000s
(*L-to-R*): Nelda, Yolanda, Rudy, Rosa, and Norma.

Rudy Nava and grandson, Randy Krinsky, 2002.

Many of the Nava cousins, c. 2005 (*L-to-R*): (*top row*) Jason Garza, Jeatonne Nava, Hector Nava, Randy Krinsky, Sean Garza, Vanessa Covarrubias, Sabrina Covarrubias, Sarina Covarrubias, Mandy Garcia, Josh Garcia, Timo Galvan, Jacob Galvan, (middle row) Rissa Krinsky, Deanna Galvan, Roanna Garcia Rihn, Freddie Lozano, Romy Nava, Stefanie Garza, Donna Garcia Tunches, Krystal Isom, (bottom row) Heather Nava, and Brandon Munoz (son of Erica Covarrubias)

Nava siblings, 2013: (*L-to-R*) Yolanda, Nelda, Rudy Jr., Norma, Hector, Rosa, and Anthony Peres.

(*L-to-R*) Rudy Jr., Hector Jr., Hector, Anthony
Peres, and Anthony Peres Jr., 2013.

Heather Nava Rollins's wedding, Rockport, July 2016:
(*L-to-R*) Romy Nava, Randy Krinsky, Stefanie Garza,
Heather Rollins, Lonnie Garcia, Roanna Garcia Rihn,
Donna Tunchez, Freddie Lozano, and Hector Nava Jr.

A gathering of Nava cousins, 2014: (*L-to-R*) Freddie Lozano, Timo Galvan, Josh Garcia, Charles Villafana (husband of Stefanie Garza), Sean Garza, Jason Garza, Hector Nava Jr., Manuel Tunchez (husband of Donna Garcia), Anthony Peres Jr., Romy Nava, Randy Krinsky, Angelo Trevino (son of Heather Nava), and Justin Tunchez (son of Donna Garcia).

Hector Nava Sr. (1952–2014), father of Hector and Heather.

The Garcia girls: (*L-to-R*) Yolanda, Roanna Garcia Rihn, Mandy, Donna Tunchez, and Deanna Garcia Galvan.

Felix and Yolanda Garcia, on occasion of their fiftieth wedding anniversary, December 2013: (*L-to-R*) Deanna, Yolanda, Felix, Roanna, and Donna.

Rhiannon Sewell's wedding, September 2016: (*L-to-R*): Krystal
Isom, Donna Tunchez, Stefanie Villafaña, Charles Villafaña, Yolanda
Garcia, Rosa Krinsky, Rudy Nava "Baby Boy," and Emma Z. Nava.

Rhiannon Sewell, Jeatonne Nava (Rhiannon's mother),
Norma Garza, Randy Krinsky, Nelda Covarrubias, Roanna Rihn,
Frances Nava, Jennifer Irving, Romy Nava,
Josh Garcia, and Juyeong Hyu Garcia.

Tunchez family: (*L-to-R*) Juyeong Hyu Garcia, Josh
Garcia, Donna, Justin, Krystal Isom, and Manuel.

Galvan family: (*L-to-R*) Jacob, Maricella, Timo,
Deanna Garcia Galvan, and Joe.

Rudy Nava Jr. family: (*L-to-R*) Beau Sewell (Rhiannon's husband),
Romy Nava, Rhiannon Sewell (daughter of Jeatonne), Rudy Jr.,
Emma, Jeatonne Nava Odom, Emma Odom (daughter of Jeatonne).

Children of Nelda Nava Covarrubias, 2009:(*L-to-R*)
Sarina, Freddie Lozano, Sabrina, and Vanessa.

Rosa Nava Krinsky, 2013.

Randy Krinsky, 2009.

Rissa Krinsky, 1994.

Traditional Family Recipes

For the Navas, family meant fellowship, food, and good times. Over the years, the family might have spread out, many leaving Rockport bound for Houston, San Antonio, Connecticut, and even Wyoming. Big family gatherings became few and far between. When it was time to come together, there was only one place to do it: Rudy and Clara's. My grandparent's home in Rockport was the central hub of family affairs and the place to be for holidays and celebrations. On the rare occasion when faraway family came back to town for a visit, that was where they could be found. When that occurred, there was always an overabundance of food. That's the one thing you can always count on our family to do—feed you!

Like many families, mine have come up with their own take on numerous household favorites that were served at the dining room table over the years. Most cooks will try to tell you that their specific recipe is the best for preparing a holiday ham or turkey; my family was no different. I won't bore you with those types of traditional family recipes. What I have listed here are a few of the more unique dishes served by Clara Nava at our family home in Rockport, or that I grew up with as cooked by my mother, Rosa Nava Krinsky. Some are still Clara's own distinctive recipes, some Rosa's unique take on traditional dishes, others handed down by relatives over the years—all delicious. Please bear in mind that many of these were taken from my grandmother's handwritten notes in her recipe book, and every effort has been made to verify that the instructions and ingredients are correct. I offer them to you with best wishes and hope that they will bring your family the same joy that they brought mine.

Momma's Faves!

Salsa Verde (Green Chili Sauce)

1/2 lb. (4–6) tomatillos (green tomatoes)
1 small white onion, diced (omit for salsa to last longer)
1 avocado, pitted and peeled
1 clove garlic
1/2 lemon or lime
4–6 serrano peppers
3 pinches of cilantro (fistful, okay)
Salt and pepper to desired taste

1. Remove husk from tomatillos and wash.
2. Remove stems from serrano peppers and wash.
3. Cook tomatillos and serrano peppers in 2–3 cups of water until swollen (do not overboil).
4. Let cool. Pour contents of pot (water, tomatillos, and peppers) in a blender. Add remaining ingredients. Liquefy.
5. May be poured in small jars to save or share with others. Be sure to refrigerate and enjoy all week! Goes great with tacos! Serves 4–6.

Cornbread Casserole

2 cans creamed corn
2 cans whole kernel corn, undrained
2 eggs
2 cups melted butter or margarine (4 sticks)
2 cups sour cream (16 oz.)
1 cup chopped onions
2 boxes Jiffy Corn Muffin Mix
1 tsp. sugar (optional)

1. Mix all ingredients together and pour in large casserole dish.
2. Bake for 1 hour at 375 °F or until bubbly and crust is brown.
3. If you thought you liked corn, wait until you taste this dish! Serves plenty!

Rosa's Cranberry Salad

24 oz. fresh whole cranberries
1 large orange, peeled, cut into wedges
1 can crushed pineapples, drained
1 cup walnuts, diced
3 stalks of celery, diced
1/2 tsp. salt
2 cups boiling water
2 pkgs. raspberry gelatin
2 cups sugar
1 large orange, peeled, cut into wedges

1. In food processor or blender, process cranberries and orange wedges, then set aside.
2. In a separate bowl, mix drained pineapple, diced walnuts, and diced celery (I process walnuts and celery for a finer cut).
3. Add salt. Add cranberry mixture. Blend well.
4. Add 2 packages raspberry gelatin and 2 cups boiling hot water, mixing well to dissolve gelatin.
5. Allow to cool for 20 minutes.
6. Meanwhile, in 1 cup water, add 2 cups sugar and heat to a boil, cooking until liquid begins to thicken. Then remove from heat and let cool for 10 minutes. Once cool, add to gelatin mixture and stir well.
7. Refrigerate entire mixture for 1 hour, or overnight, and enjoy!

8. Our family used to make this every year for the Thanksgiving and Christmas holidays to serve with turkey or ham. If there are any leftovers, you then have a small snack or dessert!

Rosa's Fideo Con Carne

A Household Favorite

12 oz. package of vermicelli
1 lb. ground sirloin, chuck, or round steak, cubed (or ground beef, if preferred)
1 can Rotel diced tomatoes and peppers
1/2 can tomato sauce
1 clove garlic
1/4 white onion
1 tsp. oregano
1 tsp. cumin
salt and pepper to desired taste
cooking oil

1. On medium heat, add enough cooking oil to frying pan to brown vermicelli, set aside.
2. In a separate large frying pan, add enough cooking oil to saute onions until glossy, then add meat. Fry ground or cubed beef until brown.
3. Add contents of Rotel diced tomatoes and peppers to the meat.
4. Add tomato sauce.
5. Mash garlic in a *molcajete*, adding a bit of water as you progress, then add to mixture.
6. Add the cumin and oregano, then salt and pepper to taste.

7. Add browned vermicelli, stir, and add enough water to cover all ingredients.

8. Cover with lid and cook on medium heat for about 20 minutes or until vermicelli is soft.

9. Serve with refried beans, sliced tomatoes, and hot corn tortillas.

Granny Smith Slaw

1/4 cup orange juice
1/4 cup plain yogurt
2 tbsp. mayonnaise
1 tbsp. lemon juice
1 tbsp. sugar
1/2 tsp. celery seed (optional)
8 oz. coleslaw mix
1 cup celery
1 Granny Smith apple, cored
1 cup seedless grapes, halved

1. In a large bowl, whisk together the orange juice, yogurt, mayonnaise, lemon juice, sugar, and celery seed (optional).
2. Add the coleslaw mix, apple, celery, and grapes, then toss gently to coat.
3. Cover and refrigerate for up to 2 days.
4. Serves 6.

Clara's Cranberry Bread

2 oranges (for juice and rinds)
3/4 cup (up-to) hot water
4 tbsp. CRISCO® shortening, melted
4 cups flour
2 eggs, beaten
2 cups sugar
2 cups cranberries, halved or dried
1 tsp. salt
2 cups walnuts
3 tsp. baking powder
1 tsp. baking soda

1. Preheat oven to 325 degrees.
2. Grease and flour two 9 inch × 5 inch loaf pans.
3. Using a small grater with small holes, grate the orange rinds.
4. Squeeze oranges into measuring cup, adding rinds and hot water, equal to 3/4 cup.
5. Sift flour, sugar, salt, baking soda, and baking powder into a medium-sized mixing bowl.
6. Combine orange juice mixture with shortening and eggs, and add to above mixing bowl.
7. Mix well.
8. Stir in cranberries and nuts.
9. Pour entire mixture into prepared loaf pans.

10. Bake for 45–60 minutes (until a toothpick comes out clean and dry).
11. Allow to cool.
12. Enjoy!

Fresh Green Fruit Salad

2 pkg. pistachio pudding
2 containers cool whip
2 apples, unpeeled and cored, chopped in small pieces
1 can mandarin oranges, drained
1 large can diced pineapple, drained
1 jar cherry halves, drained
2 bananas, sliced
1 tsp. lemon juice
1 bag miniature marshmallows
1 cup chopped walnuts

1. In a large bowl, mix the pistachio pudding powder with the cool whip.
2. In a separate bowl, toss the first five ingredients together. Add lemon juice.
3. Mix in the marshmallows and chopped walnuts.
4. Fold in the cool whip mixture. Wala!

Sweets and Treats

Clara's Strawberry-Fig Preserve

3 cups mashed figs
1 1/2 cup sugar
3 oz. strawberry gelatin
1 tsp. salt

1. Combine figs and sugar into a heavy saucepan.
2. Cook over medium heat, stirring constantly for 2 minutes.
3. Gradually stir in gelatin and cook over low heat, stirring constantly for 15 minutes.
4. Remove from heat.
5. While still hot, spoon preserves into sterile jars (fill to within a 1/2 inch from the top).
6. Remove air bubbles (agitate to settle, stir, or similar method).
7. Wipe rim of jar and cover immediately with metal lid and screw-on band.
8. Put jar in a boiling water bath (5 minutes per half pint) before storing.

Candied Pears

Growing up, Grandma Clara always had plenty of fruit preserves in the cabinet. She used only the freshest fruit, grown in her own backyard, and was happy to send you home with a jar or two! Lots of great memories!

8–10 fresh pears
pickling spice
white vinegar
sugar
cloves
cinnamon sticks
produce protector
(Amount needed of above depends on amount of water used)

1. Peel and pare pears, slice in large pieces.
2. For each 1 cup of water add the following:
   - 1/3 cup sugar
   - 1 tsp. produce protector (e.g. Fruit Fresh, to prevent browning)
3. In a pot, add pears, water, sugar, and produce protector.
4. Add enough liquid to just cover fruit (do not cover entirely).
5. Bring to a boil. Lower heat and simmer until tender (to your liking).
6. Taste. Add more liquid if not tender enough, or sugar if too tart.

7. To each quart jar to be filled with pear mixture, add the following:
   - 1 tsp. pickling spice
   - 1 tsp. white vinegar
   - 6 cloves
   - 1 cinnamon stick

Pan De Polvo

1 bag (5 lb.) Pillsbury flour
1 can (3 lb.) CRISCO shortening, melted
2 cups sugar, divided
3 tsp. baking powder
4 cinnamon sticks (more or less)
2 cups water (more or less)

1. Pulverize 2 sticks cinnamon with 1 cup sugar in processor. Set aside.
2. Bring 2 sticks cinnamon with 2 cups water to a boil. Set aside.
3. Melt CRISCO shortening in the can, over the stove. Let cool.
4. Mix flour, 1 cup sugar, and baking powder. Add melted shortening and warm cinnamon water to the flour mixture.
5. Knead but do not overwork the dough. Let rest, covered with a damp towel.
6. Spray cookie sheet with Pam.
7. Make small-sized balls out of the dough and flatten with the palm of the hand to the size of a quarter.
8. Place flattened dough balls close together on the cookie sheet since these do not expand.
9. Cook for 10-12 minutes until bottoms are tan in color.
10. Dust warm cookies in cinnamon sugar.
11. Adjust cinnamon water and cinnamon sugar, according to need.

12. These cookies are traditionally served at weddings and made at Thanksgiving and Christmas. They are commonly called Mexican wedding cookies.

Apricot Cobbler

3 sticks margarine
3 cups sugar
3 cups flour
3 tsp. baking powder
3/4 tsp. salt
3 cups milk
3–16 oz. cans of apricots (save juice)

1. Melt the margarine in an 8 inch × 8 inch baking dish. Allow margarine to cover bottom and sides of dish.
2. Prepare a thin batter by mixing together the sugar, flour, baking powder, and salt.
3. Beat in the milk.
4. Pour batter into baking dish.
5. Spread the apricots over the batter and then pour juice over the apricots.
6. Bake in oven at 350 degrees for about 45 minutes or until golden brown.

Traditional Cooking Tips
from the Nava Kitchen

- After stewing a chicken to be diced for *arroz con pollo*, casseroles, etc., let it cool in the broth before cutting into chunks—it will have twice the flavor!
- A roast with the bone in will cook faster than a boneless roast. The bone allows the heat to penetrate deep inside the roast quicker!
- Never cook a roast cold. Let it stand for an hour or so at room temperature first. Always brush with oil before and during roasting to seal in the juices.
- When boiling corn, try adding sugar to the water instead of salt; this will toughen the corn.
- To ripen tomatoes quickly, put them in a brown paper bag and place in a dark pantry. They will ripen overnight!
- Don't like the odor from cooking cabbage? Place a small tin cup of vinegar on the stove near the cabbage. This will absorb the odor.
- To keep celery crisp, try standing the stalks up in a pitcher of cold salted water and refrigerate.

¡Buen Provecho!
- The Navas

Name Index

Bibliography

"1734 Goraz Complaint on Patricio Rodriguez." In *Louis Lenz Collection* (1940). Dolph Briscoe Center for American History, The University of Texas at Austin, Box 2Q232, 1734.

Ayoub, Jack. "Flores Brothers: Texas Heroes." *The Brownsville Herald* (October 11, 2013). http://www.brownsvilleherald.com/opinion/ letters_to_editor/flores-brothers-texas-heroes/article_51606f4e-322e-11e3-9c94-001a4bcf6878.html (accessed March 28, 2017).

Barr, Alwyn. "Siege of Bexar." *Handbook of Texas Online* (June 12, 2010). http://www.tshaonline.org/handbook/online/articles/ qeb01 (accessed December 26, 2017).

Carrasco, Raphael. "Morisques et Inquisition Dans Les Iles Canaries." *Revue de L'histoire des Religions* 202, no. 4 (1985): 379–387.

Castillo, Mike M. *Wrested from This Peaceful Life: Santa Anna at the Alamo.* Lulu.com, 2008.

Chabot, Frederick C. *With the Makers of San Antonio.* San Antonio: Artes Graficas, 1937.

Chapa, Gene A. *CIDA Home Page.* n.d. http://www.cida-sa.org (accessed April 26, 2016).

"Chapter I: The Canary Islanders at Home." *Family Rodriguez.* http://www.poblar.com/Rodriguez/YanaguanaSuccessors/chapter-I.htm (accessed April 19, 2016).

"Chapter II: A Royal Decree." *Family Rodriguez.* http://www.poblar. com/Rodriguez/YanaguanaSuccessors/Chapter-II.htm (accessed April 19, 2016).

"Chapter V: Quautitlan to San Antonio de Bexar." *Family Rodriguez.* http://www.poblar.com/Rodriguez/YanaguanaSuccessors/ Chapter-V.htm (accessed April 19, 2016).

Chipman, Donald E. "Spanish Texas." *Handbook of Texas Online* (June 15, 2010). http://www.tshaonline.org/handbook/online/ articles/nps01 (accessed April 23, 2016).

———. *Spanish Texas, 1519–1821.* Austin: University of Texas Press, 1992.

Corner, William, ed. *San Antonio de Bexar: A Guide and History.* San Antonio: Bainbridge & Corner, 1890.

Cox, I. J. "The Early Settlers of San Fernando." *The Quarterly of the Texas State Historical Association* (Texas State Historical Association) 5, no. 2 (October 1904): 142–160.

Cox, Mike. "Aransas Abattoir." *TexasEscapes.com* (May 1, 2013). http://www.texasescapes.com/MikeCoxTexasTales/Aransas-Abattoir.htm (accessed April 18, 2018).

De la Teja, Jesus. *A Revolution Remembered: The Memoirs and Selected Correspondence of Juan N. Seguin.* Austin: State House Press, 1991.

De Zavala, Adina. *History and Legends of The Alamo and Other Missions In and Around San Antonio.* San Antonio, 1917.

Doughty, Robin W. *Wildlife and Man in Texas: Environmental Change and Conservation.* College Station: Texas A&M University Press, 1983.

Flannery, Tina. "Mexican Military Movements in the Texas Revolution." January 1966.

"General Austin's Order Book for the Campaign of 1835." *The Quarterly of the Texas State Historical Association* (Texas State Historical Association) 11, no. 1 (July 1907): 1–55.

Gibson, Steve. "1735 Military Roster of San Antonio de Bexar Presidio." *BexarGenealogy.com* (2002). http://bexargenealogy. com/archives/vivatejas.htm (accessed March 13, 2017).

———. "The Members of the Ramon Expedition of 1716." *Bexar Geneaology.com* (2002). http://bexargenealogy.com/archives/ramon. htm (accessed January 23, 2019).

Groneman, Bill. *Alamo Defenders, A Genealogy: The People and Their Words.* Austin: Eakin Press, 1990.

Guerra, Mary Ann N. "Naming the Town and The First Election in Texas." *University of the Incarnate Word* (1977). http://www.uiw.edu/sanantonio/NametheTown.html (accessed May 23, 2012).

———. "The First Civil Settlement in Texas." *University of the Incarnate Word* (1987). http://www.uiw.edu/sanantonio/FirstCivilSettlementinTexas.html (accessed May 23, 2012).

Guthrie, Keith. "Fulton, George Ware, Sr." *Handbook of Texas Online* (June 12, 2010). http://www.tshaonline.org/handbook/online/articles/ffu08 (accessed June 26, 2016).

Hackett, Charles W. "AGUAYO EXPEDITION." *Handbook of Texas Online* (June 9, 2010). https://tshaonline.org/handbook/online/articles/upa01 (accessed May 15, 2012).

Haneveer, Victoria. "How the Cuisine of the Canary Islands Influenced Tex-Mex." *HoustoniaMag.com* (August 9, 2016). https://www.houstoniamag.com/articles/2016/8/19/how-the-cuisine-of-the-canary-islands-is-related-to-tex-mex (accessed May 20, 2017).

Hopewell, Clifford. *James Bowie Texas Fighting Man: A Biography.* Austin, Texas: Eakin Press, 1991.

Krinsky, Rosa Nava, interview by Randy L. Krinsky. (April 26, 2012).

Levenson, Eric. "'We lost everything:' Rockport, Texas suffers major hurricane damage." *CNN* (August 26, 2017). https://www.cnn.com/2017/08/26/us/rockport-texas-hurricane-harvey/index.html (accessed January 25, 2019).

Lozano, Ruben Rendon. *Viva Tejas, The Story of the Tejanos, the Mexican-born Patriots of the Texas Revolution.* San Antonio: Alamo Press, c. 1936, 1985.

Lozano, Ruben Rendon, and Mary Ann Noonan-Guerra. "The Story of the Tejanos, the Mexican-born Patriots of the Texas Revolution." *Viva Tejas.* http://bexargenealogy.com/archives/vivatejas.htm (accessed July 22, 2018).

Maranon, Domingo. "Letter to Lord Governor Don Benito Arminan." In *H.M. Henderson Papers (1804–1903,1931), Accession 1954.* Translated by Criselda Cantu and Robert Tarin. Dolph Briscoe

Center for American History, The University of Texas at Austin (July 30, 1814).

Martinello, Marian L., and Thomas H. Robinson. *San Antonio, The First Civil Settlement in Texas: A Guide for Teachers, K-12.* San Antonio: Canary Island Descendants, 1981.

"Records of Don Manuel Angel de Villegas Puente." In *Louis Lenz Collection,* volume 724. Austin: Dolph Briscoe Center for American History, The University of Texas at Austin, Box 2Q232, 1731.

Rockport-Fulton Chamber of Commerce. "Connie Hagar Birding Nature Areas." *Rockport-Fulton Chamber of Commerce.* http://www.rockport-fulton.org/Connie-Hagar-Birding-Nature-Areas (accessed December 20, 2017).

———. *Rockport-Fulton Chamber of Commerce.* http://www.rockport-fulton.org/ (accessed December 20, 2017).

Rodriguez, Jose Maria. *Rodriguez Memoirs of Early Texas.* San Antonio: Passing Show Printing, 1913.

Rodriguez, Salvador. "Last Will and Testament of Salvador Rodriguez." In *H.M. Henderson Papers (1804-1903, 1931), Accession 1954.* Austin: Dolph Briscoe Center for American History, The University of Texas at Austin, Box 2Q232, (April 8, 1804).

Texas State Historical Association. "CANARY ISLANDERS." *Handbook of Texas Online* (June 12, 2010). http://www.tshaonline.org/handbook/online/articles/poc01 (accessed 10 2019, February).

Texas State Library and Archives Commission. *Texas Declaration of Independence* (December 5, 2017). https://www.tsl.texas.gov/treasures/republic/declare-01.html (accessed December 12, 2019).

The Lighthouse Inn at Aransas Bay. *The Lighthouse Inn at Aransas Bay* (2015). http://www.lighthousetexas.com/history-en.html (accessed June 26, 2016).

U.S. Army Center of Military History. "71st Infantry Division—Order of Battle of the United States Army—WWII—ETO." *U.S. Army Center of Miltary History.* https://history.army.mil/documents/ETO-OB/71ID-ETO.htm (accessed March 11, 2019).

Waymarking. "The Flores de Abrego Family and Floresville." *Waymarking* (January 13, 2007). http://www.waymarking.com/ waymarks/WM14NT_The_Flores_de_Abrego_Family_and_ Floresville (accessed March 13, 2017).

Weber, David J. *The Spanish Frontier in North America.* New Haven: Yale University Press, 1992.

Endnotes

Chapter 1

1 (Weber 1992, 155)
2 (Weber 1992, 160)
3 (Weber 1992, 163)
4 (Chipman, Spanish Texas, 1519–1821 1992, 117)
5 (De Zavala 1917, 8)
6 (Chipman, Spanish Texas 2010)
7 (Chipman, Spanish Texas, 1519–1821 1992, 133)
8 (Weber 1992, 188)
9 (Chipman, Spanish Texas, 1519–1821 1992, 135)
10 (Texas State Historical Association 2010)
11 A *cabildo* was a Spanish colonial town council.
12 (Chapter I: The Canary Islanders at Home n.d.)
13 (Chapter II: A Royal Decree n.d.)
14 (Chapter II: A Royal Decree n.d.)
15 (Chapter II: A Royal Decree n.d.)
16 (Texas State Historical Association 2010)
17 A *jáquima*, or hackamore, is a bridle without a bit, working by exerting pressure on the horse's nose.
18 (Records of Don Manuel Angel de Villegas Puente 1731)
19 An adze is a cutting tool used for carving or shaping wood.
20 A *comal* is a type of sandstone griddle.
21 "Records of Don Manuel Angel de Villegas Puente," 1731, Box 2Q232, Volume 724 Louis Lenz Collection, Dolph Briscoe Center for American History, The University of Texas at Austin, pp 21-23, 32-33.
22 (Chapa n.d.)
23 Panniers are boxes or leather containers used to carry heavy loads.
24 (Corner 1890, 127)
25 (Chapter V: Quautitlan to San Antonio de Bexar n.d.)

[26] (Corner 1890, 127)

[27] (Chapa n.d.)

[28] (Guerra, The First Civil Settlement in Texas 1987)

[29] (Guerra, Naming the Town and The First Election in Texas 1977)

[30] (Chipman, Spanish Texas, 1519–1821 1992, 139)

[31] (Chipman, Spanish Texas, 1519–1821 1992, 140)

[32] (Chipman, Spanish Texas, 1519–1821 1992, 145)

[33] (Guerra, Naming the Town and The First Election in Texas 1977)

Chapter 2

[34] (Gibson, The Members of the Ramon Expedition of 1716 2002)

[35] (Chabot 1937, 166)

Chapter 3

[36] (Martinello 1981)

[37] (Haneveer 2016)

[38] "Plazas of San Antonio, as they existed in 1778, compiled by John Ogden Leal, undated," General Map, Poster, and Broadside Collection, MS352, University of Texas as San Antonio Libraries Special Collections.

[39] Close-up of San Antonio Plaza, 1778.

[40] (Records of Don Manuel Angel de Villegas Puente 1731)

[41] Moriscos of the Canary Islands were different from the Moors of Europe. These were not the descendants of Iberian Muslims but instead were Muslim Moors taken from northern Africa in Christian raids or pirate attacks. In the Canary Islands, they were both freed and enslaved Moriscos gradually converting to Christianity. Some served as guides in raids against their former homelands. Once the king forbade these raids, the Moriscos lost contact with their old religion of Islam. They later became a large part of the island population, eventually accounting for half of the inhabitants of Lanzarote alone. Unfortunately, they were often subjected to ethnic discrimination. Though Goraz was known to be of dark complexion, it is unknown to the author if he was indeed of Morisco origin or if the use of this term was meant merely as a derogatory slur.

[42] It is important to note that Arocha often signed documents on behalf of municipal officials as many of them could not write well. The harshness of frontier life usually meant that education was not a priority. Many of the *alcaldes* who served could not write or sign their names.

[43] A curate is a person charged with the care of, or duty to cure for, the souls of the parish, such as a parish priest, or more specifically to this case, possibly an assistant to the vicar.

44 (I. Cox 1904, 157)

45 (1734 Goraz Complaint on Patricio Rodriguez 1734)

46 (S. Rodriguez 1804)

47 Transcription and subsequent translation courtesy of Subject Matter Expert Translation, LLC.

48 The original document has a letter that is illegible. It could be the number 50 or the letter *R*, followed by the words *roille* or *oille*, neither of which are found in the dictionary nor is there any phonological approximations of these words. Given the context, it is logical to think that the illegible character is the number 50, and that the word *oille* refers to a type of yoking animal.

49 It is unclear if the will refers to carts used for farming or to carriages. For consistency, the word *cart* is used throughout the translation.

50 *La plasita* appears to refer to part of the ranch that was denoted by this name.

51 The almud was a measurement of the land needed to grow certain grains.

52 A vara is an old Spanish unit of length, which varied in size at various times and places.

53 The third part of the testator's wealth that he was, by law, to bequest to his children.

54 The fifth part of the testator's wealth that he was able to freely bequeath to whomever he wanted, even if he had children.

55 A bequest left in addition to the "third and fifth."

56 It is unclear if "for the road" refers to a working horse or to a saddle horse.

57 "Alcalde ordinario" was in the absence of a corregidor, the presiding officer. Usually there were two alcaldes, "de primer voto" (first vote) and "de segundo voto" (second vote), being the first vote superior over the second vote.

58 In the original document, the word *vecinos* ("neighbors") is inserted in between the lines.

59 In this instance, the actual document says, "entre renglones y vecinos," literally "in the between the lines and neighbors."

60 (Maranon 1814)

61 Translation courtesy of Cristela Cantú and Robert Tarín.

Chapter 4

62 Texians were residents of Mexican Texas and, then, the Republic of Texas. Today, the term is used more specifically to differentiate early Anglo settlers of Texas, especially those who supported the Texas Revolution.

63 Texas-born citizens of Mexico with Spanish ancestry.

64 (Hopewell 1991, 100)

65 (Barr 2010)

66 The Consultation was the provisional Texian government during the Texas Revolution, October 1835–March 1836.

67 (Texas State Library and Archives Commission 2017)
68 (General Austin's Order Book for the Campaign of 1835 1907)
69 (Castillo 2008, 38)
70 (Flannery 1966, 41, 60)
71 (De la Teja 1991, 80, 187)
72 (J. M. Rodriguez 1913, 13)
73 (Gibson, 1735 Military Roster of San Antonio de Bexar Presidio 2002)
74 (De la Teja 1991, 118)
75 (De la Teja 1991, 116)
76 (De la Teja 1991, 44, 94–95, 117)
77 (Groneman 1990, 99)
78 (Ayoub 2013)
79 (Waymarking 2007)

Chapter 5

80 (Rockport-Fulton Chamber of Commerce n.d.)
81 (M. Cox 2013)
82 (Guthrie 2010)
83 (M. Cox 2013)
84 (M. Cox 2013)
85 (The Lighthouse Inn at Aransas Bay 2015)
86 (Doughty 1983, 176)
87 (Doughty 1983, 181)
88 (Rockport-Fulton Chamber of Commerce n.d.)
89 (The Lighthouse Inn at Aransas Bay 2015)
90 (Levenson 2017)

Chapter 6

91 (U.S. Army Center of Military History n.d.)
92 A *molino* is a traditional corn grinder or, in this case, the building where the corn was ground and tortillas made.
93 *Buelita* is what we called our grandmother, or "abuelita," for short.
94 *Pan dulce*, "sweetbread," (c'mon, you know this!)
95 *Curanderas*, in Spanish or Latin culture, are healers who solely use folk remedies.

About the Author

Born the maternal grandson of Rudy Nava Sr., Randy Krinsky grew up in Houston but spent many weekends and vacations enjoying visits to Rockport, Texas. He would listen to his grandmother's stories of family history and ancestral relations. His mother, Rosa Nava Krinsky, would expand on her mother's tales by sharing her genealogical studies with Randy, exploring ancestor histories and shedding light on family mysteries.

After a career in law enforcement and then project management, Randy returned to school and earned degrees in history and English. He discovered his passion for writing and began a second career as a writer. He began writing on the topics of film theory, history, and pop culture, being published in both magazines and websites. It was then that he was urged to take a short family history essay, written to win a college scholarship, and expand it into book form. What followed was years of research, built upon his mother's initial studies, which began back in 2000. He visited archives and museums, raided family journals and photo albums, until ultimately compiling it all into his first book, *Uncertain Destiny*.